The Greening of Hebrews?

The Greening of Hebrews?

Ecological Readings in the Letter to the Hebrews

Jeffrey S. Lamp

☙PICKWICK *Publications* · Eugene, Oregon

THE GREENING OF HEBREWS?
Ecological Readings in the Letter to the Hebrews

Copyright © 2012 Jeffrey S. Lamp. All rights reserved. Except for brief quotations in critical publications or reviews, no part of this book may be reproduced in any manner without prior written permission from the publisher. Write: Permissions, Wipf and Stock Publishers, 199 W. 8th Ave., Suite 3, Eugene, OR 97401.

Pickwick Publications
An Imprint of Wipf and Stock Publishers
199 W. 8th Ave., Suite 3
Eugene, OR 97401
www.wipfandstock.com

ISBN 13: 978-1-61097-655-8

Cataloging-in-Publication data:

Lamp, Jeffrey S.

The greening of Hebrews? : ecological readings in the letter to the Hebrews / Jeffrey S. Lamp.

xii + 134 p. ; 23 cm. — Includes bibliographical references and indexes.

ISBN 13: 978-1-61097-655-8

1. Bible. N.T. Hebrews—Criticism, interpretation, etc. 2. Human ecology in the Bible. I. Title.

BS2775.52 L25 2012

Manufactured in the U.S.A.

New Revised Standard Version Bible: Catholic Edition, copyright 1989, 1993, Division of Christian Education of the National Council of the Churches of Christ in the United States of America. Used by permission. All rights reserved.

Chapter 2, "Creational Christology: Recovering the Christological Voice of Creation (Hebrews 1:2–3a)," is a modified version of an article I published as "Creational Christology: A Rationale for Wesleyans to Care for the Created Order," *Wesleyan Theological Journal* 44 (Spring 2009) 91–103. Used by permission. All rights reserved.

*To my grandchildren, Jonah, Kadin, and Emily,
with hope for a more sustainable future,
and to their grandmother, my wife, Monica,
who gave me the encouragement
to see this project through to its completion.*

Contents

Acknowledgments · ix

List of Abbreviations · xi

1 Introduction · 1

2 Creational Christology: Recovering the Christological Voice of Creation (Hebrews 1:2–3a) · 10

3 What's With Cutting up All Those Animals? Reading the Sacrifice of Christ in Hebrews from the Perspective of the Animals · 21

4 The Promise of God's Rest (Hebrews 4:1–11): Joshua, Jesus, Sabbath, and the Care of the Land · 37

5 A Whispered Voice in the Choir: Toward an Ecological Pneumatology in Hebrews · 51

6 "He Has Prepared a City for Them" (Hebrews 11:16): Escapist Eschatology or Ecological Expedience? · 69

7 "We Have an Altar" (Hebrews 13:10): The Reclamation of the Eucharist for Ecological Responsibility · 85

8 Creational Christology Redux: Angels, Torah, Son, and Creation (Hebrews 2:1–4) · 101

9 Conclusion · 113

Bibliography · 119

Author Index · 125

Ancient Document Index · 127

Acknowledgments

I WOULD LIKE TO thank Norm Habel for giving me the chance to embark upon this project by granting me that first opportunity to explore ecological hermeneutics with my first paper at the San Diego meeting of the SBL. I extend my gratitude to all of the members of and participants in the Consultation on Ecological Hermeneutics, especially those who gave encouragement and feedback on my first and subsequent presentations, as well as to those who attended sessions at meetings of the Wesleyan Theological Society and Society for Pentecostal Studies, whose faces often donned quizzical expressions as I guided them through this way of encountering the biblical text. I offer a deep sense of appreciation to my friend, the chairperson of the Undergraduate Theology Department at Oral Roberts University, Dr. Edward Watson, and to the Dean of the College of Theology and Ministry, Dr. Thomson Mathew, for their administrative support and tenacity in securing travel funding so that I might attend those conferences where this project took form. I also thank them and all those involved in granting me the sabbatical leave in the Spring 2010 semester where the manuscript finally came to completion. And to Justin Smith, a former student and friend, a hearty thanks for serving as my research assistant during my sabbatical. I hope this book proves worthy of their input.

Abbreviations

1 *Clem.*	1 *Clement*
1 Cor	1 Corinthians
1 *En.*	1 *Enoch*
1 Pet	1 Peter
1QH	*Thanksgiving Hymns*
1QS	*Rule of the Community*
1 Sam	1 Samuel
2 *Bar.*	2 *Baruch*
2 Cor	2 Corinthians
2 *En.*	2 *Enoch*
4 Macc	4 Maccabees
4QFlor	*Florilegium*
ANET	Ancient Near Eastern Texts Relating to the Old Testament. 3rd ed. Edited by James B. Pritchard. Princeton: Princeton University Press, 1969
Ant.	Josephus, *Jewish Antiquities*
Apoc. Mos.	*Apocalypse of Moses*
b. Menaḥ.	Babylonian Talmud, Menaḥot
b. Yoma	Babylonian Talmud, Yoma
b. Zebaḥ.	Babylonian Talmud, Zebaḥim
Bar	Baruch
BDAG	Walter Bauer, Frederick W. Danker, W. F. Arndt, and F. W. Gingrich. *Greek-English Lexicon of the New Testament and Other Early Christian Literature.* 3rd ed. Chicago: University of Chicago Press, 2000
CD	Cairo Genizah copy of the *Damascus Document*
Col	Colossians
Creation	Philo, *On the Creation of the World*
Deut	Deuteronomy
Diogn.	*Diognetus*
Eccl	Ecclesiastes

Eph	Ephesians
Exod	Exodus
Fug.	Philo, *De fuga de inventione*
Gal	Galatians
Gen	Genesis
Hag	Haggai
Heb	Hebrews
Herm. *Sim.*	Shepherd of Hermas, *Similitudes*
Hos	Hosea
Isa	Isaiah
Jer	Jeremiah
Jub.	*Jubilees*
KJV	King James Version
Leg.	Philo, *Legum allegoriae*
Lev	Leviticus
LXX	Septuagint
Matt	Matthew
Mic	Micah
Migr.	Philo, *De migratione Abrahami*
m. Soṭah	Mishnah, Soṭah
NEB	New English Bible
NIV	New International Version
NRSV	New Revised Standard Version
NT	New Testament
Num	Numbers
OT	Old Testament
Plant.	Philo, *De plantatione*
Prov	Proverbs
Ps	Psalm
Rev	Revelation
Rom	Romans
RSV	Revised Standard Version
SBL	Society of Biblical Literature
Sib. Or.	*Sibylline Oracles*
Sir	Sirach
Somn.	Philo, *De somniis*
Spec. Laws	Philo, *On the Special Laws*
Wis	Wisdom of Solomon

1

Introduction

WHERE IT ALL STARTED

WHEN I FIRST INFORMED a class of undergraduate students at Oral Roberts University that I would be using an upcoming sabbatical leave to complete work on this book of ecological readings of portions of Hebrews, one of them quipped, "So you're working on the greening of Hebrews?" After the laughter subsided, I took the bait and walked headlong into the perennial student ploy of distracting the professor from the day's tasks to pursue a rabbit trail. Unlike in many of these transparent attempts, however, there developed a higher than normal degree of interest as I proceeded in my description of this project. Some of this interest derived from a heightened concern among this demographic for matters environmental. But beyond this, they were intrigued by the prospect that there might a hermeneutical approach to the Bible specific to this concern. So my students succeeded that day in their quest to divert me from my lesson plan, but in the process, many of them were exposed to new horizons of reflection on a topic dear to their hearts.

What follows is a collection of studies that began as a series of paper presentations in the Society of Biblical Literature (SBL) Consultation on Ecological Hermeneutics. My first work with this Consultation came in November 2007 at the San Diego meeting. The paper was a conscious effort to explore this hermeneutic in a rather wooden manner in order to ascertain its value in my own work in the broader field of ecotheology. The paper met with positive feedback and constructive criticism from those in attendance, and upon further reflection on this experience, I decided that ecological hermeneutics would prove a valuable resource in my professional and academic pursuits.

2   THE GREENING OF HEBREWS?

It was then that I hit upon the present project. I would continue to present papers in the Consultation as well as in other academic societies (the Wesleyan Theological Society and the Society for Pentecostal Studies), exploring Hebrews through this ecological hermeneutic. Why Hebrews? At first, simply because the passage that caught my attention for my first paper happened to come from Hebrews: "but in these last days he has spoken to us by a Son, whom he appointed heir of all things, through whom he also created the worlds. He is the reflection of God's glory and the exact imprint of God's very being, and he sustains all things by his powerful word" (Heb 1:2–3a).[1] But as I worked on that initial presentation I discovered that there were several features that made a broader investigation of this biblical book through an ecological hermeneutic an intriguing prospect.

SO WHY HEBREWS?

Anyone who has consulted the standard New Testament introductions or the numerous commentaries on Hebrews is confronted immediately by the dizzying array of unanswered questions of critical introduction surrounding this text. Virtually every conceivable question is capable of multiple plausible solutions, each finding some warrant either in the text of Hebrews itself or in the history of its interpretation. Beginning with the question of authorship, then extending into such matters as audience, provenance, date, occasion, purpose, and theological and philosophical background, scholarship has produced few certain results. Even the matter of the genre of the book generates significant discussion.[2] This uncertainty makes complex the task of more traditional biblical commentary. But for reasons that will become clear below, the lack of certainty in these areas is not a significant obstacle for this hermeneutic, and in fact, may actually be of liberating effect in its application. Lack of definitive an-

---

1. Unless otherwise noted, all quotations are from the New Revised Standard Version (NRSV).

2. A survey of introductory works, commentaries, and specialized studies debate the genre of Hebrews, typically identifying it in three broad categories: epistle, homily, or rhetoric. The designation chosen in our study will be "letter-sermon," for it adequately captures the literary features evident in the book. That it is a largely hortatory work is undisputed. The part of our designation we will call "sermon" captures both the homiletical purpose and the rhetorical strategies used to develop the hortatory flavor of the book. "Letter" accounts for both the epistolary postscript (13:20–25) and the traditional view that Hebrews was circulated as a letter.

swers to these matters of critical introduction allows for an interaction with the text predominantly in terms of the text itself. With a paucity of unequivocal data regarding the origin and setting of Hebrews, we may pursue a reading free from the encumbrances of speculative reconstructions that by necessity render tentative any conclusions derived from them. Engagement with the text will proceed from data ascertained from the text itself.[3] Obviously there will arise need to address some of these matters in the course of reading Hebrews, particularly in terms of, for example, the nature of the dualism/dualities present in the argumentation, but the outcomes of an ecological reading of Hebrews are not dependent on a precise identification of influences behind the text. This is because the ultimate goal of ecological hermeneutics is to read the text from the perspective of Earth—understood as the total scope of nature of which human beings are a part—and not to create the kinds of readings that produce scholarly biblical commentary.

In other words, ecological hermeneutics, as we will define it, is an ideological hermeneutic. The goal is not to get at the meaning of the text, if by that we mean understanding the text as a literary product whose composition was conditioned by a myriad of historical, social, intellectual, and other factors. Rather, the goal is to hear a suppressed voice, the voice of Earth, in, through, or even against the text. We will proceed with a confidence that the text will provide sufficient clues toward understanding its basic message and that speculation beyond this will not appreciably assist in our particular ideological agenda. From a practical standpoint, this means we will not here rehash the endless academic debates over matters of critical introduction, information readily available elsewhere, though we will, throughout our studies, discuss such matters where they are directly pertinent to the topic at hand.

Another reason for choosing Hebrews for these discussions is due to its reputation, deserved or not, that it puts forth a "spiritualized" vision of Christian thought. As we will observe in the studies, a significant strategic and rhetorical interest of the author is to compare symbols from the old covenant to the Son in such a way as to relativize their current significance or to re-interpret them in terms of final, superior fulfillment in the Son. Frequently this comparison is couched in language of an earthly

3. This is the approach taken by Schenck in his study of the backgrounds of the cosmology and eschatology of Hebrews. For his rationale and methodology, see Schenck, *Cosmology and Eschatology*, ch. 2.

versus heavenly dichotomy that posits ultimate significance and value to heavenly, eternal, and spiritual realities over against earthly, temporary, and created realities. Put starkly, if an ecological hermeneutic, as we will define it, can produce plausible readings that argue for the integrity and intrinsic value of Earth in such a presentation, then it may reasonably do so in less apparently hostile biblical texts. As an epilogue to this point, it may be that an ecological reading such as we will pursue might challenge our perceptions that Hebrews is actually that "otherworldly" in orientation after all.

So these are the reasons for choosing Hebrews as the target text for the application of an ecological hermeneutic. We now turn our attention to the substance of this ecological hermeneutic itself.

ECOLOGICAL HERMENEUTICS DEFINED[4]

The development of ecological hermeneutics is in large measure connected to the work of biblical scholar Norman C. Habel.[5] A significant stage in the development of the hermeneutic was the work of several writers in the Earth Bible Project. The final product of this group of writers, the Earth Bible Series, consisted of five volumes of studies sampling texts covering the whole canon of the Christian Bible.[6] The team of writers had several aims in view with this project:

- to acknowledge, before reading the biblical text, that as Western interpreters we are heirs of a long anthropocentric, patriarchal, and androcentric approach to reading the text that has devalued the Earth and that continues to influence the way we read the text;

- to declare, before reading the text, that we are members of a human community that has exploited, oppressed, and endangered the existence of the Earth community;

---

4. This section summarizes Habel, "Introducing Ecological Hermeneutics," 1–8.

5. For a summary of the work leading to this Consultation, including the publication of the Earth Bible Project, see Habel, "Origins and Challenges," 141–59.

6. Entries in the series include Habel, *Readings from the Perspective of Earth*; Habel and S. Wurst, *The Earth Story in Genesis*; Habel and Wurst, *The Earth Story in Wisdom Traditions*; Habel, *The Earth Story in Psalms and Prophets*; Habel and Balabanski, *The Earth Story in the New Testament*.

- to become progressively more conscious that we are also members of the endangered Earth community in dialogue with ancient texts;
- to recognize Earth as a subject in the text with which we seek to relate empathetically rather than as a topic to be analyzed rationally;
- to take up the cause of justice for Earth and to ascertain whether Earth and the Earth community are oppressed, silenced, or liberated in the text;
- to develop techniques of reading the text to discern and retrieve alternative traditions where the voice of Earth and Earth community has been suppressed.[7]

To achieve these aims a series of six principles was developed in consultation with ecologists:

- *The principle of intrinsic worth:* the universe, Earth, and all its components have intrinsic worth/value.
- *The principle of interconnectedness:* Earth is a community of interconnected living things that are mutually dependent on each other for life and survival.
- *The principle of voice:* Earth is a subject capable of raising its voice in celebration and against injustice.
- *The principle of purpose:* the universe, Earth, and all its components are part of a dynamic cosmic design within which each piece has a place in the overall goal of that design.
- *The principle of mutual custodianship:* Earth is a balanced and diverse domain where responsible custodians can function as partners with, rather than rulers over, Earth to sustain its balance and a diverse Earth community.
- *The principle of resistance:* Earth and its components not only suffer from human injustices but actively resist them in the struggle for justice.[8]

---

7. Habel, "Introducing Ecological Hermeneutics," 1–2.
8. Ibid., 2.

These principles were subsequently subjected to critique and analysis, leading to the conclusion that a more radical revisioning was necessary to produce a reading of the Bible that was not simply about Earth, nature, or creation, that is, a reading where Earth is not simply a thematic interest of the Bible,[9] but rather where Earth is a speaking subject in biblical texts. Since 2004, the Consultation on Ecological Hermeneutics at the annual meetings of the SBL has worked to define, refine, and explore a hermeneutic that utilizes three criteria—suspicion, identification, and retrieval—in recovering the voice of Earth in the Bible.

The criterion of *suspicion* sees traditional readings of a text as inherently anthropocentric, or perhaps originating from an anthropocentric bias. As human beings, particularly within Western cultural traditions, we often see ourselves as of a separate order of being with respect to the other than human order. Such a perspective objectifies the rest of nature, relegating it to the status of a means toward achieving human ends. In the reading of biblical texts, this bias asserts itself in interpretations that diminish the value of nature as a subject of intrinsic value in its own right. Rather, the interests of human beings predominate the reading of biblical texts, with the place and voice of the rest of the cosmos ignored and frequently suppressed. The next element of an ecological hermeneutic is that of *identification*. Here interpreters empathize with the other than human created order, recognizing their own deep connections with the world. Once the suspected anthropocentric biases are identified within a text, readers must come to grips with their kinship with Earth in order to become more sensitive to the voice of Earth. The final facet of this hermeneutic is that of *retrieval*. Having identified anthropocentric biases and developed identification with the created order, the interpreter now seeks to discern how creation speaks when its voice has either been suppressed or ignored, or understood as mere poetic symbolism.

Many of the studies from the Consultation have been collected and published in the volume *Exploring Ecological Hermeneutics* (2008).

This hermeneutic has much in common with other ideological readings of the Bible, such as feminist and post-colonial hermeneutics. And as with any form of ideological reading of the Bible that involves suspicion in its approach, there is a danger that the resulting reading is so shaped by suspicion that the biblical text may be dismissed as a conversation partner.

---

9. This is more the approach taken by *The Green Bible*.

In my own appropriation of the hermeneutic in the present project, my goal is to be more nuanced in its application, unapologetically identifying the biases of the text but equally unapologetically seeking for Earth's constructive voice wherever possible. There will indeed be times where our study will reveal Earth's voice announcing its pain in the face of injustice and calling prophetically for the establishment of right relations between the human and other than human partners in creation. Sometimes the object of this prophetic critique of Earth will be human interpretations of the text; at other times it will be the text itself.

A significant strength of this hermeneutic is the insistence that suspicion not become an end in itself, but rather that it lead the interpreter into an empathy with Earth that sensitizes the reader to hear the voice of Earth where it has been muted in favor of other concerns of the biblical authors or subsequent interpreters. Moreover, my own application of the hermeneutic draws on other interpretive approaches that mitigate the prospect that suspicion might run unbridled throughout our studies. First, the ecological hermeneutic highlighted here will utilize intertextuality in its application. Frequently in the course of this volume appeal will be made to other scriptural traditions as we strive to articulate the voice of Earth. Canonical context will assist in tempering the potential for the studies to devolve into a rigid hermeneutic of suspicion by reading the passages under investigation within the larger fabric of the biblical story.

Coupled with this intertextual reading will be a limited theological reading of the Bible. A burgeoning field in its own right with many specific manifestations in its application, theological interpretation generally revolves around two major foci. First, theological interpretation stipulates that one appropriate goal in reading the Bible is that it informs the theological traditions of its readers. While this book will stop short of articulating a systematic theology for ecologically responsible living in the world, many of the specific instances of Earth's voice will vocalize a sense of "ought" in terms of faith and practice. Another aspect of theological interpretation that will impinge on these studies is the appropriation of certain strands of subsequent Christian tradition in reading the passages. Those familiar with the language of "theological interpretation" will understand that one aspect of this approach is the utilization of various creedal and doctrinal formulations within Christianity as starting points, or lenses, through which to interpret biblical texts. At certain points throughout these studies, such an approach will prove helpful in uncovering the voice of Earth. Given that Hebrews is part of the Christian scriptural tradition, it is appropriate to assess the history of its subsequent interpretation within the broader scope of Christian tradition and to bring these considerations to bear in the process of reading Hebrews from an ecological perspective.

These adjustments notwithstanding, the structure of the discussions in this volume will closely follow the three-fold model of the ecological hermeneutic described above. The primary focus of the book is the rigorous application of the hermeneutic to Hebrews; various other interpretive tools, including more traditional forms of exegesis, will be brought into service of the ecological hermeneutic. We now turn our attention to the map that will guide our studies.

CONTOURS OF THE BOOK

First, a caveat as to what this book is not. It will not, as stated earlier, be a rigorous commentary on Hebrews. Even if one were to argue for the desirability of a specialized ecological commentary on the letter-sermon, the coverage evidenced in this series of studies is far from comprehensive, with some small sections of the text receiving significant discussion, other larger sections receiving cursory overview, and other stretches not addressed at all. The studies undertaken here draw on certain texts as points of departure for the trek to uncover the voice of Earth as it pertains to issues of ecological significance suggested but not developed in the rhetorical concerns of the author. In summary, the resulting discussions will tend toward a study of ecological themes drawing impetus from anchor points in the text.

Moreover, this book will not produce a systematic theology or ethic of creation care. As noted earlier, the voice of Earth will frequently emerge with prophetic tones that clearly suggest appropriate responses from the community of readers. However, beyond summarizing and synthesizing the results of these studies, there will be no fully blown constructive system developed. That will have to wait for another day.

Finally, this book will not be an exercise in exegesis traditionally understood. We will certainly make use of some of these tools, but neither the approach nor the result will resemble those rigorous exercises occupying the attention of so many of us in those glory days of graduate school.

In positive terms, this book will consist of a series of seven studies employing the ecological hermeneutic developed by the Consultation on Ecological Hermeneutics in the SBL in order to ascertain the muted voice of Earth on several topics as suggested in the argumentation of Hebrews. Some of the studies uncover Earth's voice in terms of some rather lofty theological issues: creation and christology, pneumatology, and eschatology. Other studies are much more mundane by comparison: animal rights, land care, and liturgical observance. By way of a thesis, an ecological reading of Hebrews demonstrates that, despite the rhetorical concerns of the author, embedded in the argument are textual clues, derived primarily from the christological affirmations of the argumentation, that connect Hebrews with the larger biblical concern for the integrity and care of the created order.

As we hinted at earlier, there is no shortage of studies that address the Bible in terms what it has to say *about* Earth, creation, or nature. There is much of value in these studies. However, to borrow the title of Norm Habel's recent book, on this head the Bible often proves to be "an inconvenient text."[10] One image that Habel develops in this book is the identification of "green" texts and "grey" texts. Green texts are those that are clearly positive in terms of their affirmation of the value and care of creation. Grey texts, on the other hand, are those that show how human beings and/or God despoil or disregard Earth in favor of their own ends. The biblical witness concerning the integrity and value of creation is less than unambiguous on occasions. What is needed is a hermeneutic that can read the whole of the Bible, both the convenient and inconvenient passages, from the common vantage point of Earth's perspective, such that the cry of Earth, both in celebration and in protest, might receive a clear hearing among the Bible's human audiences. At times, what is needed is a way to identify green shoots poking up through the grey expanse of some biblical texts. By virtue of its apparently other-worldly or spiritualized presentation, Hebrews is a text that might be identified as a largely grey text. The present study will seek for those green shoots in Hebrews so that we might hear the voice of Earth speaking through the text.

---

10. Habel, *An Inconvenient Text*.

2

Creational Christology

Recovering the Christological Voice of Creation
(Hebrews 1:2–3a)

INTRODUCTION

FOUND IN THE NEW Testament are several texts of a high christology that attribute in some way the creation of the cosmos to the creative agency of Christ or the Son. Most prominent of the texts of what I call "creational christology" are John 1:10; 1 Cor 8:6; Col 1:16–17; Heb 1:2–3a; and Rev 3:14. Moreover, the passages from Colossians and Hebrews expand upon creative agency by attributing the active and ongoing sustenance of the cosmos to Christ or the Son. The focus of all of these passages, in part, is to establish Christ or the Son as the rightful Lord of all, the one to whom allegiance is due.

Our focus in this discussion is to examine one of these passages—Heb 1:2–3a—as paradigmatic for reading all of the passages identified in the trajectory of creational christology for the specific purpose of hearing the voice of Earth in the midst of the exalted christological accolades in the passage.[1] To this end we will employ the three principles developed

---

1. Scholars are not unanimous that Heb 1:2–3a speaks of the Son as the agent of creation. Schenck, *Cosmology and Eschatology*, 139–42, argues that elsewhere in Hebrews God is identified as the creator of the universe (cf. 2:10; 3:4; 4:3; 11:3), and that in 1:2–3a Christ functions as a metonymy for God's purpose in creation, which is for Christ to be God's redemptive logos and wisdom in creation. This understanding of 1:2–3a derives from Schenck's reading of Hebrews that concludes that the created order was always inferior and destined for destruction once it served its purpose in the redemption of human beings. Jewett, *Letter to Pilgrims*, 22, takes a slightly different tack. He notes that that which is identified as made by the Son are the Aeons (Gk. *aiōn*), a word that has

10

and explored in the Consultation on Ecological Hermeneutics of the Society of Biblical Literature. Using the principles of suspicion, identification, and retrieval, we will adopt the point of view of the created order in reading this passage as we seek to hear its voice in this text.

SUSPICION

The text with which we are presently concerned, Heb 1:2–3a, reads as follows:

> But in these last days [God] has spoken to us by a Son, whom [God] appointed heir of all things, through whom [God] also created the worlds. He is a reflection of God's glory and the exact imprint of God's very being, and he sustains all things by his powerful word.

We suspect that the voice of Earth has been sublimated by two parties. The first of these is the biblical author. The passage occurs as foundational to the author's agenda of advocating the supremacy of the Son over against the significant symbols of Judaism. Creative agency is cited as one of the first evidences that the Son is initiating a better covenant than the old one. So creation serves as a datum in the author's agenda rather than as a subject worthy of its own consideration.

The second party that has neglected the voice of creation in Heb 1:2–3a is the community of subsequent interpreters. Not only have they followed suit with the biblical author's agenda, but they have frequently mined the passage for its contributions to christology, particularly in defense of the doctrines of the pre-existence and divinity of the Son—the concerns of Trinitarian theology. Again, creation serves as a datum, this time in service of a significant arena of doctrinal development in Christian theology.

The primary bias against creation here is not in favor of anthropocentrism proper, but rather in favor of the ideological agendas of interest

---

among its meanings reference to "the world as a spatial concept" (BDAG 33), but that Jewett takes literally to refer to the spiritual entities spoken of in Colossians (cf. 1:26) in light of his hypothesis that Hebrews was addressed to the Lycus Valley and thus addresses the type of exigence that gave rise to Colossians. However, Jewett comes around to seeing the referent as the universe: "The aeons, therefore, lose their threatening and demonic qualities and at the same time assume the character of an ordered universe instead of a collection of independent cosmic systems, each answerable to its own peculiar exigencies" (23).

to human beings. As such, in this passage the voice of Earth is not so much actively suppressed as it is passively ignored. The argument of the letter-sermon quickly builds momentum with its singular focus on the supremacy of the Son such that any inclination to stop and reflect on the perspective of Earth is steamrolled in service of the author's agenda, an inclination followed by those embroiled in the christological controversies of the first few centuries of Christian history. In fact, the composition and history of interpretation of Heb 1:2–3a is emblematic of many theological tendencies to sacrifice the voice of the other than human created order to address more relevant doctrinal matters.[2]

IDENTIFICATION

Though christology seems to be center stage here, the text of Hebrews itself gives a clue for the identification with creation through its very christological affirmations. But here we must go beyond ch. 1 into ch. 2 to observe this clue. In Heb 2:6–7 the writer makes appeal to Ps 8:4–6 [5–7 LXX] to begin to make the case that via the incarnation the Son has identified with the plight of mortal human beings in order to bring them to glory.

Psalm 8, though in large part a commentary on Gen 1, particularly Gen 1:26–28, and thus falling prey to the same anthropocentric bias identified and critiqued by Habel,[3] does make a strong affirmation of the fingerprint of God in the created order (Ps 8:3), an affirmation perhaps reinforced by the *inclusio* of vv. 1 and 9 that identifies Earth as the stage on which God's name is extolled.[4] The psalmist cries out in hymnic praise of the wonder of a God whose power is seen in the vastness and beauty of the cosmos, but who also cares for seemingly insignificant humanity. Indeed, through the citation of Ps 8, the writer of Hebrews plays on what is clearly an anthropocentric bias—human beings as the pinnacle of God's creative work—in order to provide the rationale for the Son's

---

2. This was recently seen in the attempts by several prominent members of the National Association of Evangelicals (NAE) to remove Richard Cizik from his post in the organization for his advocacy of an environmental agenda. This agenda was deemed by many to detract from the NAE's focus on more "relevant" issues such as abortion and gay marriage. See the article by Cooperman, "Evangelical Angers Peers," A04.

3. Habel, "Playing God," 33–41.

4. Though see Carlay, "Psalm 8," 111–24.

incarnation.[5] To those who know the Psalm, however, the citation of vv. 4–6 elicits remembrance of v. 3, and thus provides opportunity for the voice of Earth to be injected into the argument of Hebrews at this point. And here the voice of Earth might remind us that Gen 1:26–28 is not the only extant tradition on the creation of human beings. There is also Gen 2:7, which links human beings to Earth via their creation from the dust of the ground.

It is at this point that identification with creation is evident. The same human physicality birthed from Earth is the stuff that the Son shared in his incarnation (Heb 2:14).[6] In effect, the incarnation is one of the strongest affirmations of the intrinsic worth not only of human beings, but also of the whole of creation. It is thus one of the strongest affirmations of the connection of human beings to Earth.

So here is the punch line. In the midst of a discussion that highlights the anthropocentric focus of the Son's redemptive work, the writer of Hebrews, in all likelihood inadvertently, provides the means through which human beings might identify with Earth. When listened to with a discerning ear, the very essence of the christology of Hebrews, at least to this point of the letter-sermon, not only affirms that all of creation—in its origins and sustenance—is within the purview of christology, but also speaks to the unity of all aspects of that creation—human and other than human alike. To use language more at home in Trinitarian theological reflection, both the pre-existence and incarnation of the Son provide the framework for envisioning the identification of human beings with the rest of the created order. The creative agency of the Son in his pre-existence brings forth Earth, from which in turn come human beings; the incarnation of the Son from the stuff of Earth serves as the bridge that identifies human beings with Earth, affirming the intrinsic worth of both in the process.

RETRIEVAL

In the context of our discussion of Heb 1:2–3a, we have confirmed the suspicion that the place of creation in the author's argument has been that of a datum in christological formulations, indicating a preference for

---

5. So Craddock, *Hebrews*, 37.

6. The Johannine Prologue also draws together the creative agency of the Logos with the incarnation (cf John 1:10, 14).

issues deemed relevant to the author's agenda to the exclusion of those relevant to creation. And we have seen that despite this interest of the author, the very development of the argumentation itself has opened the way for human identification with Earth through the discussion of the Son's incarnation. We now seek to determine just precisely what the content of Earth's voice might be in this passage.

At the outset of our discussion, we might offer a preliminary suggestion as to what the voice of Earth would say were it heard in concert with the author's christological statements. Perhaps it might say, "I can assist human beings in their quest to know God's Son more fully." We will expand on this later, but for now, it gives us a starting place and some direction for the following reflections.

As we noted earlier, the author of Hebrews offers the creative agency of the Son as a datum informing a high christology. Our suggestion goes beyond this strategy to include the notion that creation is a source of knowledge informing that christology. In other words, creation itself has much to teach us toward the development of a more fully orbed understanding of the person and work of the Son. So the question remains: how do we go about retrieving Earth's voice toward this end? We will use the concept of wisdom as the vehicle for this retrieval.

It is virtually axiomatic that in Jewish thought, wisdom theology is creation theology.[7] In the Hebrew Bible, Prov 3:19–20 and 8:22–31 describe the role of God's wisdom in the creation of the world. This gives rise to the notion that implanted within the structures of creation itself is the very wisdom of God. The creative means provides a sort of logic for the order of the universe. As a result, the study of God's creation gives insight into the character of God, particularly in terms of the wisdom of God, which is displayed and played out on the stage of the world. Those who devote themselves to the study of God's creation in order to learn of God and the ways of God are designated as wise. In short, there is a sapiential deposit found within and learned from creation because creation is ordered on the basis of God's wisdom.

Of special pertinence for the present discussion is a passage in the pseudonymous work from post-biblical Judaism, the Wisdom of Solomon. The primary text of interest is 7:22—8:1:

---

7. Representative of the voluminous literature in this regard are Murphy, *Tree of Life*, 118–21; Clifford, "Hebrew Scriptures," 507–23; Levinson, "Observations," 43–57.

7:22 [F]or wisdom, the fashioner of all things, taught me.
There is in her a spirit that is intelligent, holy,
unique, manifold, subtle,
mobile, clear, unpolluted,
distinct, invulnerable, loving the good, keen,
irresistible,
23 beneficent, humane,
steadfast, sure, free from anxiety,
all-powerful, overseeing all,
and penetrating through all spirits
that are intelligent, pure, and altogether subtle.
24 For wisdom is more mobile than any motion;
because of her pureness she pervades and penetrates all things.
25 For she is a breath of the power of God,
and a pure emanation of the glory of the Almighty;
therefore nothing defiled gains entrance into her.
26 For she is a reflection of eternal light,
a spotless mirror of the working of God,
and an image of his goodness.
27 Although she is but one, she can do all things,
and while remaining in herself, she renews all things;
in every generation she passes into holy souls
and makes them friends of God, and prophets;
28 for God loves nothing so much as the person who lives with wisdom.
29 She is more beautiful than the sun,
and excels every constellation of the stars.
Compared with the light she is found to be superior,
30 for it is succeeded by the night,
but against wisdom evil does not prevail.
8:1 She reaches mightily from one end of the earth to the other,
and she orders all things well.

This passage is a paean to the highly personified figure of Lady Wisdom that is widely seen by commentators to have exerted an influence on Heb 1:2–3a.[8] Pseudo-Solomon leads into this song of praise by

---

8. E.g., Attridge, *Hebrews*, 40–42; Bruce, *Hebrews*, 47–48; Craddock, *Hebrews*, 23; Johnson, *Hebrews*, 67–68; Koester, *Hebrews*, 187; Lane, *Hebrews* 1–8, 12–13. We must be careful to note, however, that the present argument is not predicated upon the direct influence of Wisdom upon Hebrews. The matter of the influence of Wisdom upon the NT is complicated by the date of composition of Wisdom. Dating Wisdom is somewhat difficult, with proposals ranging from as early as the mid-first century BCE to the mid-first century CE. Affinities with the thought of Philo and the circumstances of Alexandrian

acknowledging the role that Wisdom played in his acquisition of knowledge pertaining to the "structure of the world" (7:17), which includes knowledge of such things as astronomy, meteorology, and zoology (vv. 18–20), in other words, things of the natural order. The assertion that Wisdom was the "fashioner of all things" (v. 22) grants her the qualifications to instruct him on these matters. This Wisdom has not only fashioned the universe; she also pervades and penetrates "all things" (v. 23), renews "all things" (v. 27), and orders "all things" well (8:1). Moreover, she is "a reflection of eternal light/a spotless mirror of the working of God/ and an image of [God's] goodness" (7:26). She inhabits the souls of holy persons and makes them friends of God (v. 27), and such persons are characterized as those who live with Wisdom (v. 28).[9]

Several similarities are observable between Wis 7:22—8:1 and Heb 1:2–3a.[10] The most obvious and pertinent are the attributions of creative agency to both Wisdom (Wis 7:22) and the Son (Heb 1:2) and the continuing sustenance of the cosmos to both (Wis 7:23, 27; 8:1; Heb 1:3).[11] Wisdom is a "reflection" of the light, works, and goodness of God (Wis 7:26), while the Son is the "reflection" of God's glory (Heb 1:2). The word for "reflection" is the same Greek word in each passage (*apaugasma*),

---

Jews in the early first century have led some to place the date of composition around the time of the pogrom against the Jews under Caligula (e.g., Winston, *Wisdom of Solomon*, 20–25). For our purposes, the matter of influence is not important; it is sufficient to note that "common phraseology and ideas are general enough to suggest that they arise from common concerns and values rather than from literary dependence," Kolarcik, *Book of Wisdom*, 440; cf. Lane, *Hebrews 1–8*, 12.

9. For a broader discussion of the relationship of Wisdom to the created order, see Bergant, "Wisdom of Solomon," 138–50; and Turner, "Spirit of Wisdom," 113–22.

10. Fee, *Pauline Christology*, 595–619, severely criticizes those who advocate a "wisdom christology" that sees Christ patterned after the personified figure of Lady Wisdom. Moreover, he critiques the use of the Wisdom of Solomon as background to Pauline thought (613–18). Granted, he does not address his critique explicitly toward Hebrews (nor does he argue for Pauline authorship of Hebrews), but he does critique such application in passages like 1 Cor 8:6 and Col 1:16–17, which are quite similar to Heb 1:2–3a. We are not arguing for a "wisdom christology" per se, but rather for analogies that might help in our understanding of Heb 1:2–3a. O'Brien, *Hebrews*, 53–54 suggests that rather than direct influence of Wisdom on Hebrews at this point, perhaps a better characterization of the relationship is that they both originate from a similar religious milieu.

11. Buchanan, *Hebrews*, 7–8, argues that Heb 1:3 does not speak to the Son's sustenance of the universe by his word, but rather that he exercises legal authority over the universe on the basis of God's word. But the similarity of depiction of the Son with Wisdom seems to argue against this view.

providing a lexical as well as conceptual link between the references. However, the Son is further designated as the "exact imprint of God's very being" (v. 2), which is an advancement upon the description of Wisdom. Nevertheless, at the level of detail and conceptualization, Wisdom and the Son are depicted in quite similar terms.

The net effect of these similarities is that Wisdom and the Son are to be viewed alike in terms of their respective connections to the created order. This is seen particularly in their roles in creating and upholding the universe.[12] As we look back at the thumbnail sketch of Wisdom in Wis 7:22—8:1, we observe the convergence of two facets of Wisdom's activity, one in the cosmos and one among humanity: "Wisdom is God's activity in the cosmos and in humanity that renews the earth and restores human beings."[13] This understanding draws together in terms of Wisdom the observations we made in our discussion of identification with Earth in terms of the Son. Wisdom brings together Earth and humanity; the Son, by becoming human, does the same thing.

In the Book of Wisdom, Wisdom is portrayed in a vividly personified manner that draws attention to her activity in the world. In the larger context of Jewish wisdom traditions, while the Wisdom of Solomon certainly innovates upon the depictions of Wisdom in the biblical traditions, and even upon the rather conservative depiction of Wisdom in the post-biblical Sirach,[14] it does retain the sense that one comes to know Wisdom by virtue of interacting with her as she performs her activity in the world. And given the similar portraits of Wisdom and the Son we have observed, a further similarity is suggested. In the way that God's wisdom is discerned in the created order, so too may God's Son be discerned in the created order. Wisdom theology sees the imprint of divine wisdom in creation; Heb 1:2–3a suggests the imprint of God's Son in creation.[15]

---

12. Philo attributes the function of upholding the universe to the Logos (*Migr.* 6; *Plant.* 8; *Fug.* 112).

13. Kolarcik, *Book of Wisdom*, 505.

14. For an analysis of this innovation, see di Lella, "Conservative and Progressive Theology," 139–54.

15. The idea of the divine image in creation has antecedents in Greek thought. Plato states that the world is the image of a perceptible deity, characterized by unsurpassed greatness, beauty, and perfection (*Timaeus* 92C). In Hellenistic Jewish thought, Philo asserts that "the image [*eikōn*] of God is the Word [*logos*] through which the whole world was constructed" (*Spec. Laws* 1:81). In light of Philo's understanding of the Logos, this seems to suggest that in some sense the created order bears the image of God.

So what does this similarity in depictions of Wisdom and the Son have to do with the retrieval of Earth's voice in Heb 1:2–3a? We began this discussion with the suggestion that Earth might say to us that it can point us toward the Son. We might envision Earth crying out in the tenor of Lady Wisdom in Prov 1:20: "the Son calls out in creation, through me he raises his voice." We will now conclude this discussion of retrieval with some potential examples of the content of this voice as suggested by this study.

There are three areas in which Earth might speak, all framed within the context of the commonality shared between the human and other than human components of creation. First, Earth might emphasize that it is itself an object of God's care and benevolence. Both human beings and the cosmos in general bear the divine imprint. Hebrews 1:2–3a as elucidated by Wis 7:22—8:1 shows us that the creative agency and ongoing upholding of all of creation renders creation as the special object of God's concern. The Son, and Lady Wisdom before him, reflect something of God's glory and goodness, and in the sense that the Son and Wisdom are the beloved of God, so too is that with which the Son and Wisdom are involved, and for the purposes of this discussion, that entails the birthing and maintaining of creation. The creation tradition of Gen 1 affirms the goodness of both human and other than human orders of creation. Hebrews 1:2–3a simply reminds us that based on our *common origins* in the creative agency of the Son, the other than human creation has a claim to the same divine benevolence as do human beings.[16]

Second, the voice of Earth reminds us that the incarnation of the Son embodies the *common experience* of human and other than human

---

In an interesting verbal link, Philo (*Plant*. 50) states that the world is a "reflection of holiness, a copy of the original" (*hagiōn apaugasma, mimēma archetupou*). The term *apaugasma* links together the ideas of the world and Wisdom as a reflection of the divine from Hellenistic Judaism with the notion from Hebrews that the Son is a reflection of God. World, Wisdom, and the Son are all identified as reflecting something of the divine, affirming the created order as that from which knowledge of God is derived.

16. Koester, *Hebrews*, 185–86, suggests that Heb 1:1–2 brings together two ideas, God's final word in the Son and God's initial creative word, through the use of Jewish wisdom categories. The net effect of this connection is the understanding that God's purposes for people and creation cannot be separated: "All things were created by God and exist for God, and the end of all things is revealed in the Son through whom God made the universe." Koester also adds, "God's purposes for humankind are carried out within the scope of [God's] purposes for the world [God] created through the Son." See also Johnson, *Hebrews*, 66.

creation in the present. We argued earlier that the incarnation of the Son, his embodiment in the same stuff of Earth from which human beings are created, serves as a strong connection between human and other than human creation. Human beings share life with other than human creation to such a degree that to speak of human beings living a disinterested existence with respect to the rest of creation is ludicrous. In Rom 8:18–25 Paul links together the current experience of human suffering with that of the whole of creation. Creation groans longing for release from its bondage; human beings groan longing for the redemption of their decaying bodies. But here we must note that the Son who serves as the point of human identification with creation further defines this connection through his own suffering, serving as a bridge between the suffering of human and other than human creation in his suffering. So as its voice is heard, Earth points us to the suffering Son who binds us to it, and shows us that we have a vested interest in empathizing with a world that shares the pains of life with us.

Third, and deriving from the previous two observations, Earth claims its place in the redemptive work of the Son. Again, the incarnation of the Son is instructive here. If in his death he procures for human beings release from the bondage and fear of death on the basis of his sharing of flesh and blood with them (Heb 2:14–15), then the connection of human beings to Earth strongly suggests that the stuff from which human beings are made is itself the object of redemption as well. And indeed, this is affirmed elsewhere in the New Testament, most notably in Rom 8:21 where Paul explicitly links together the redemption of creation with the redemption of the children of God. The whole of creation, human and other than human alike, came into being through the creative agency of the Son and is likewise continually sustained by his power. This same Son also provides for human and other than human creation a *common destiny*, redemption from death and decay.

In short, perhaps what Earth might say to human beings is that an appropriate means of honoring the Son is to honor the world he created and sustains. The popular eschatology of a segment of contemporary Christianity holds that in the end, God will destroy the world, and given this, care for the world in the present, and here we should read the derogatory slur "environmentalism," is not warranted and is ultimately a waste of resources that should go toward evangelizing human beings. Another segment shuns environmental activism on the grounds that God will redeem creation in the end, so why bother working at it now? In answer to both of these positions, Earth might well respond, "If part of current Christian practice is to care for human beings as those for whom the Son died as they await the redemption of their bodies, then ought not human beings presently care for all that falls within the scope of his redemptive mission?"

CONCLUSION

The foregoing study has certainly not been a thorough exegesis of Heb 1:2–3a in any traditional sense of the word. Rather, the passage has served to provide some parameters for a series of observations. We observed that Earth's voice has been overlooked in the author's pursuit of a christological rather than creational agenda. Nevertheless, we also saw that the development of the author's christological argument into ch. 2 provided the means by which human beings identify with Earth, namely through the incarnation of the Son who bore the same flesh and blood as humans who were formed from Earth. Via the connection with Jewish wisdom traditions, seen in the similarity of depiction with Wisdom in Wis 7:22—8:1, the voice of Earth summons human beings to see the other than human creation as co-sharers of the imprint of the Son and of divine benevolence and ultimately redemption.

In the final analysis, the approach pursued in this discussion is probably somewhat representative of how the aforementioned passages in the trajectory of "creational christology" might be addressed.[17] It is my hope that this discussion will foster further reflection on the connections between creation and christology as well as on the effort to read Scripture from the point of view of Earth.

---

17. Previous studies include a series of articles on the Johannine Prologue, Habel, "An Ecojustice Challenge," 76–82; Wainwright, "Which Intertext?," 83–88; Balabanski, "John 1," 89–94; and a study on the Colossians poem, Balabanski, "Critiquing Anthropocentric Cosmology," 151–59.

3

What's With Cutting up All Those Animals?

*Reading the Sacrifice of Christ in Hebrews
from the Perspective of the Animals*

INTRODUCTION

EARLY IN MY DAYS of reading the Bible, I came across the book of Leviticus. As one new to the reading of Scripture, I was unaware of the role of this book in the Pentateuchal narrative, its place in the cultus of Israel, and its contribution to the christology of the NT. To my untrained eye, it just looked to me to be nothing more than the book of the bloody mess. Now many years have passed, I have come into contact with learned discussions of the aforementioned issues, but still I am left with a couple questions. First, just why is the almighty God of the universe so interested in articulating meticulous directions for cutting up birds? And second, is all this detail really intrinsic to the logic of reality?

The author of Hebrews deals with this cutting up of animals in a way that reinterprets the practice in terms of christology. So while the author may not answer my first question, at least directly, the author does answer the second: indeed, cutting up all those animals is intrinsic to the logic of reality. And so is revealed the author's bias. The huge loss of animal life in the cultus is bypassed in favor of the author's christological agenda. The author of Hebrews speaks for Christ and for human recipients of his sacrifice, but who speaks for the animals?

This study will uncover the voice of animal creation in a strand of argumentation in Hebrews, particularly Heb 9:11—10:18, that articulates the doctrine of the sacrifice of Christ. The letter-sermon develops the assertion that a perfect sacrifice was necessary to procure the benefits of the forgiveness of sins for human beings. The rationale for this argument in part lies in the inadequacy of the sacrificial system of the old covenant.

The voice of animal creation will be heard in three ways. First, it will respond to the critique of the inadequacy of the "blood of goats and calves" to secure the very thing that it was allegedly initiated to accomplish, namely, pardon for sins. The writer of Hebrews concludes that their sacrifice was inadequate. The animals respond in the protest that they are the innocent victims in the human drama of sin and redemption, and to critique them is to diminish them for their role in a system not of their own device.

Second, animals affirm that they are also the implicit beneficiaries of the sacrifice of Christ. Though the author of Hebrews has an anthropocentric focus in these discussions—human beings are the explicitly identified beneficiaries of the efficacious sacrifice of Christ—the fact is that animals need no longer be sacrificed for human benefit; they are in effect "saved" by Christ's sacrifice. Of course, this is a somewhat trivial understanding of "salvation," but it points to the larger notion of salvation that I have earlier argued includes the other than human creation as the object of God's redemption.[1]

One final way in which the voice of the animals is heard is in the call for human identification with other than human animals. Here extrapolations from the preceding senses of the voice of animals in connection with other scriptural considerations make the case that genuine existence as human beings in God's world must entail a sense of identity with the rest of the animal kingdom.

THE BIBLICAL DEPICTION OF ANIMALS

The biblical traditions portray an ambivalent estimate of animals. They are seen in terms of the goodness of their initial creation as well as in terms of submission to and exploitation by human beings. An exhaustive survey of the biblical depictions of the value of animals lies beyond the scope of this discussion. But one need merely look at the portrayal of animals in Genesis and a few other references to see the full range of the valuation of animals in the biblical drama.

1. See ch. 2 above.

In the opening chapter of Genesis, God brings into existence those creatures whose home is water, sky, and ground (vv. 20–25), with the stamp of approval, "And God saw that it was good" (vv. 21, 25). With the appearance of human beings into the world, however, is introduced the complicated interrelationship between human beings and the other than human animal world. In 1:26–27 human beings are made in the image and likeness of God with the mandate, earlier given to animals, to multiply in the earth, but additionally, to have dominion over the animals. While biblical scholars have disagreed over whether the language of dominion implies that human beings are to exercise divine care in responsibility for the earth and its inhabitants[2] or that it implies a forceful rule that serves to elevate human beings to a position of superiority over the rest of creation,[3] many throughout Christian history and in more recent popular Christianity have seen in the passage a justification for human use of animals in any way that benefits human beings.[4] In the creation account of Gen 2, the first human being is brought forth from the ground (v. 7), and subsequently, in an effort to provide the human with a suitable partner, God brought forth from the earth all the animals and presented them to the human for naming (vv. 18–19). The human is given a privileged position via the naming of the animals, but among them was not found a suitable partner (v. 20). So even in the goodness of the pre-sin phase of the narrative are found the seeds for diminution of the animal kingdom.

The first death recorded in Genesis in response to the first human sin is not that of a human being, but apparently of an animal, when God made garments of skins to cover the nakedness of the offending man and woman (3:21). Abel apparently sacrificed animals from his flock to God (4:4). God's judgment against wicked humanity in ch. 6 brought with it judgment against animals as well (6:7),[5] though God's preservation of Noah's family entailed the preservation of a remnant of the animal kingdom (7:2–3). In the aftermath of the flood, God establishes a covenant with Noah that includes the animals as beneficiaries (9:8–16),[6] but at this

2. E.g., von Rad, *Genesis*, 196; Fretheim, *Genesis*, 346.
3. E.g., Habel, "Playing God," 39.
4. This tendency is noted by Wade, "Ethics of Animals," 202.
5. In *Jubilees*, the sins of the Watchers affected animals as well as human beings in terms of corruption and sin (5:2), necessitating their destruction in the flood (5:4, 20; cf. *Apoc. Mos.* 11:2–3).
6. *Jubilees* states that after the flood, both animals and human beings were given new natures so they might believe as God intended (5:12).

time God also permits human beings to exercise such dominion over the animals as to inspire fear and dread of humans and to allow human beings to eat animals for food (9:2–3). God makes the covenant with Abram, signified by the passing of the fire pot and flaming torch between the separated carcasses of an array of animals (15:7–21). And Abraham is provided a ram to sacrifice instead of his son Isaac (22:13). This rapid survey of Genesis demonstrates, again, an ambivalent view of the value of animals in the biblical record.

Such a pattern is repeated elsewhere in the Hebrew Bible as well as in the NT. Torah demonstrates a concern for the well-being of animals, providing for the relief of stray and overburdened donkeys (Exod 23:4–5), establishing them as beneficiaries of Sabbath rest (Exod 23:12; Deut 5:14), and granting them access to the produce of farmland, vineyards, and olive orchards at rest during the Sabbath year (Exod 23:11). However, a significant aspect of the Mosaic legislation is the preparation of animals as the fuel for the engine of the sacrificial cult. In the NT, in the same verse Jesus can affirm God's concern for the ravens by feeding them while maintaining the superior worth of human beings (Luke 12:24). Paul's exegesis of Deut 25:4 in 1 Cor 9:9–10 ("You shall not muzzle an ox while it is treading out the grain") maintains that this command was written entirely for the sake of human beings, affirming his right as an apostle to receive benefit from his work, and not for the poor laboring ox. Yet he can also maintain that all creation, presumably animals included, will find redemption eschatologically (Rom 8:19–23).

This sketch provides the conceptual context for the anthropocentrically biased critique of animal sacrifices given by the author of Hebrews in Heb 9:11—10:18. It is to this critique that we now turn our attention.

THE INADEQUACY OF ANIMAL SACRIFICES IN HEBREWS 9:11—10:18

In Heb 9:11—10:18 the author discusses the sacrifice of the Christ as the climax to the larger discussion of the superiority of the new covenant to the old begun in 8:1. The author frames the discussion with the citation of Jeremiah's prophecy of the new covenant God would make with the houses of Israel and Judah, quoting at length Jer 31:31–34 [38:31–34 LXX] in Heb 8:8–12 and excerpting from vv. 33 and 34 in Heb 10:16–17. This discussion of the new covenant in turn builds upon the discussion in Heb 7 of the superiority of Jesus' priesthood, patterned along the order of Melchizedek, to that of the Levitical order. In Heb 9:11—10:18, the author continues the rhetorical strategy of arguing for the superiority of the Son to various figures and institutions of Judaism employed from the beginning of the letter-sermon.

Hebrews 9:1–10 serves as the contextually immediate statement of the problem addressed in 9:11—10:18. Here the author notes that the perpetual ritual sacrifices of the priests and the annual sacrifice of the high priest on the Day of Atonement each function as an extended "parable" (v. 9) that exposes the fatal flaw of such sacrifices: they cannot perfect the consciences of the worshiper. They deal only with external matters until "the time comes to set things right" (v. 10). But it is at this point that the author betrays a fundamental axiom of his argument in 9:11—10:18. As Johnson notes, "[the author] makes the 'perfecting' of the worshiper (singular, not plural) the implied goal of the cult (=religion). This is in tension with the implied goal of the cult according to Scripture, which was a state of 'at-one-ness' between God and the people of Israel considered as a whole."[7] In other words, the author of Hebrews employs a polemical argument that reframes the stakes of the issue in terms foreign to the original cultic setting for the express purpose of demonstrating how the cult falls short.[8]

With this inherent weakness of the sacrificial cult laid bare, the author begins an extended argument that demonstrates the superiority of the blood that Christ offers as the perfect high priest in the heavenly sanctuary to the blood of animals offered by merely human priests in the earthly sanctuary that is but an imperfect sketch of the heavenly. This inferior sacrifice is explicitly caricatured as "the blood of goats and calves" in 9:12, as "the blood of goats and bulls" along with the mention of "the ashes of a heifer" in v. 13, as "the blood of calves and goats" in v. 19, and

---

7. Johnson, *Hebrews*, 226. For further discussion of the premises and goals of the sacrificial system, see pp. 25–26.

8. Koester, *Hebrews*, 414, states the matter differently: "If Christ's death is the way in which God deals with sin, then the author concludes that other means—including Levitical sacrifices—must be inadequate." The presupposition of the author's argument, according to Koester, is Christ's sacrifice. Given this, there must be an inadequacy with the animal sacrifices. This provides Koester with the framework for understanding these sacrifices as a "foreshadowing" of Christ's—only with Christ's sacrifice do we understand that the Levitical sacrifices are shadows of the coming reality (cf. 427).

"the blood of bulls and goats" in 10:4.[9] The first reference in 9:12 occurs in a comparison that identifies the blood offered by Christ the perfect priest as his own blood that procures eternal redemption. The reference in v. 13 is part of a *qal wahomer* argument that concedes that if the animal sacrifices provided ritual purification for people, purification in the flesh, then "how much more" will the blood of the unblemished Christ offered through the eternal Spirit purify the consciences of worshipers to worship the living God. The reference in v. 19 occurs in the somewhat convoluted argument begun in v. 15 in which the word play on the Greek *diathēkē*, which may mean both "covenant" and "will," leads to the conclusion that even the Torah states that purification and forgiveness required the shedding of blood, a concession that simply sets up the argument that heavenly realities require better sacrifices. And the reference in 10:4 confirms the frequent refrain that the fact of continual repetition of animal sacrifices itself demonstrates their inefficacy and thus the need for a once-for-all sacrifice that purifies those who are sanctified (cf. vv. 10, 14).

Crucial to the author's strategy is the citation and exegesis of Ps 39:6–8 (LXX) in Heb 10:5–10. This citation brings together the preceding argumentation by providing the scriptural warrant for the assertions made about Christ's sacrifice. Commentators have widely noted that the author is firmly established in the tradition of the OT prophets and their critique of the sacrificial system (e.g., Isa 1:10–13; Jer 7:21–24; Hos 6:6; Amos 5:21–26; Mic 6:6–8; cf. 1 Sam 15:22).[10] Though similar, the substance of the two critiques contains a significant difference. The prophetic critique charges the people with a failure to live in obedience to the commandments of God while performing sacrificial rituals, indicating God's preference for obedience. However, the prophetic critique does not explicitly speak to the inefficacy of the sacrificial cult in itself, but only that such sacrifices do not procure their intended results when deeper covenantal obligations are being neglected.[11] In Hebrews, however, the words cited from Ps 39 are placed on the lips of Jesus in such a way as to draw a marked distinction between the external sacrifices of the old covenant

---

9. There are other references to offering animal sacrifices that do not explicitly mention the animals thus sacrificed (e.g., 5:1, 3; 7:27; 9:7, 9, 25; 10:1, 3, 8–9, 11; 13:11). The implicit unfavorable comparison to the sacrifice of Christ is nevertheless present in varying degree.

10. E.g., Johnson, *Hebrews*, 252–53; Craddock, *Hebrews*, 115.

11. Johnson, *Hebrews*, 253; O'Brien, *Hebrews*, 350 n. 42.

that displease God and the internal response of obedience Christ lives as he offers his one-time sacrifice for the perfection of the conscience.[12] In effect, the prophetic critique allows for the maintenance of the integrity of the sacrificial cult, while in Hebrews the blood of sacrificial animals is simply unable to perform what is truly necessary, that is, in the estimation of the author of Hebrews, namely forgiveness of an individual's sins and the cleansing of an individual's conscience. This is not to say that the prophetic tradition gave any greater voice to the perspective of the animals, but that the institution as such was not denigrated in terms of its intrinsic efficacy. Said another way, what we see in the Hebrew Bible is primarily a prophetic critique of the people; what we see in Hebrews is a christological critique of the sacrificial cult. The author's handling of Ps 39 brings about this transposition of focus.[13]

At this point we see the biases of the author of Hebrews emerge. Clearly the author puts forth primarily a christological bias, arguing the superiority of Christ's sacrifice over against the sacrificial cult of which the animals are a significant part. An anthropocentric bias is equally as evident, for human beings are the designated beneficiaries of the sacrifice of Christ. It is difficult, however, to determine whether the author is consciously attempting to denigrate animals in this argument, but the rhetorical effect of the argumentation moves in this direction in two ways. First, the sacrificial cult is the assumed religious backdrop of the author's understanding. As noted earlier, the Bible depicts an ambivalent estimate of the value of animals, particularly in terms of how animals are frequently exploited for human ends, and this is seen most vividly in the sacrificial cult. The author of Hebrews simply assumes this role and status for animals without protest. So the author's argument is another datum in the biblical record of the ambivalent assessment of the value of animals.

The second way in which the argument denigrates animals is found in the way the author frames the comparisons between the sacrificial cult

---

12. Johnson, *Hebrews*, 251.

13. Buchanan, *Hebrews*, 166–67, portrays the author's logic as "watertight" given his presuppositions: sinlessness is possible and is God's will; God's will would be realized; the old covenant sacrifices were not effective; therefore God has a different plan; this plan is not found in the Pentateuch but in the Psalms and prophets; the Psalms and prophets prohibited sacrifices and promised a new covenant; this new covenant required a body instead of levitical offerings; the body of Jesus provided a once-for-all sacrifice; this sacrifice of Jesus is eternally effective and provides a cleansed conscience and the forgiveness of sins.

and Christ's sacrifice. As noted above, rather than speaking exclusively in generic terms of the sacrifices offered under the old covenant, the author characterizes the sacrifices as "the blood of goats and calves" or the like. In this way of speaking, it is very easy to slide from a comparison of sacrifices to a comparison of the sources of the blood in the sacrifice, in other words, to a comparison of animals to Christ. Who comes out favorably in such a comparison is obvious.

The criterion of suspicion has uncovered christological and anthropocentric biases in the author's discussion of the superiority of Christ's sacrifice to the animal sacrifices of the old covenant. But as I have suggested in the previous chapter, even within the christologically biased argumentation of Heb 1:2-3a resides the voice of the other than human creation awaiting retrieval. It now remains to retrieve the voice of the other than human animals that lies implicit within the argumentation of Heb 9:11-10:18.

A RETRIEVAL OF THE VOICE OF ANIMALS IN HEBREWS 9:11—10:18

The voice of animals in this section of the letter-sermon consists of a three-fold interest: the response of animals to the critique of the sacrificial cult; the establishment of animals as the objects of Christ's redemptive work; and the identification of animals with human beings.

The Response of Animals to the Critique of the Sacrificial Cult

The response of animals to this critique might proceed in two ways. At one level, they might respond that the author of Hebrews has been less than fair in the strategies employed to argue for the inefficacy of their sacrifices. On the one hand, they might argue that the exegesis of Ps 39 tendentiously reassigns the responsibility for the critique of the sacrificial cult from human failure to live obediently their covenantal obligations to the inefficacy of the blood of animals to forgive sins. Among the instances of the author's redaction of the psalm is the phrase "you have taken no pleasure" (*ouk eudokēsas*) in 10:6, in reference to burnt and sin offerings, for the original "you have not required" (*ouk ētēsas*), as well as the identification of the body of the obedient one in the psalm with

Jesus.¹⁴ The net effect casts human beings into the role of the victim of sin's consequences rather than as those who, in the prophetic critique, are the active perpetrators of sin. The problem becomes, in Hebrews, not human disobedience, but rather an inadequate remedy for the sin-laden conscience. On the other hand, animals might argue that the author of Hebrews unfairly frames the intention of the sacrificial cult in terms congenial to the author's own interests.¹⁵ Of course the sacrifices of animals will not purify an individual's conscience because that simply was not the purpose of the cult in the old covenant.¹⁶ The author of Hebrews, in single-minded focus on the contours of his christological argument, has forgotten that the sacrificial cult was initiated by God in the first place.

Another response of the animals to the critique of the sacrificial cult might simply be a protest to the effect that animal sacrifice is a divinely sanctioned means provided for human beings to enable them to approach God in ritual holiness, all necessitated by human sinfulness. Animals are

---

14. See Johnson, *Hebrews*, 250–52, for discussion of the use of the psalm in the argumentation of 10:5–10.

15. Several commentators have identified how the author downplays the inherent worth of animals. Lane, *Hebrews 9–13*, 242–43, argues that what is in view in 9:15–18, where the author is typically understood to be making a play on words where the Greek term *diathēkē* may mean both "covenant" and "will," is not a play on legal terms, but rather an exposition of OT covenantal procedure, where ratification of a covenant involved pronouncing a curse upon oneself when swearing to comply with the terms of the covenant. The ratifying party was represented by animals designated for sacrifice. The bloody dismemberment of representative animals signified the violent death of the ratifying party if he proved faithless to the oath (e.g., Gen 15:9–21; Exod 24:3–8; Ps 50:5; Jer 34:17–20). Moreover, Lane notes that the term in Heb 9:22, *haimatekchusia*, is best translated "application of blood" in concert with biblical sources (e.g., Exod 29:12; Lev 4:17, 18, 25, 30, 34; 8:15; 9:9 LXX) and rabbinic sources (*b. Zebah.* 6a; *b. Menah.* 93b; *b. Yoma* 5a), which focuses on blood as the means of atonement, rather than as "shedding of blood" as in such translations as the RSV, NEB, and NIV, which places emphasis on the death of the animal (246).

16. Johnson, *Hebrews*, 249, says of this difference in goals: "The purpose of this language [in 10:1–4], to be sure, is to assert that the cult based on the law was only a shadow and not the reality, and therefore was not efficacious—by the measure, I must again insist, of the author's own understanding of the cult's goal, which is not one shared by Torah. . . . Ritual cleansing worked to prepare a people for participation in the public cult of Israel and to 'approach God' in the earthly sanctuary. But only if the conscience is cleansed from the 'awareness of sins' are people morally capable of approaching the living God." Koester, *Hebrews*, 416, comments: "Levitical sacrifices purified those who were defiled so that they could reenter the community. Christ's sacrifice leads to service that builds up the community where it fosters committed service to the afflicted."

required to give their lives in fulfillment of a contract made without their consent and for no fault of their own. At the very least, criticizing the animals for their inability to secure certain benefits for human beings smacks of crass under appreciation for the benefits they did provide.[17]

Animals as the Objects of Christ's Redemptive Work

Animals may also assert their voice by observing that they, too, are recipients of Christ's redemptive work. The sacrifice of Christ, as argued by the author of Hebrews, secures the benefits of forgiveness of sins and a perfected conscience for human beings. However, the animals may well note that by virtue of Christ's sacrifice, the blood sacrifices of animals are no longer necessary. In effect, those animals whose blood would have been required to perpetuate the sacrificial cult have had their lives spared by Christ. Though it is possible that animal sacrifice was continuing in Jerusalem at the time of the composition of Hebrews, this does not diminish the point that in the new covenant economy, the sacrifice of Christ renders obsolete the need for animal sacrifice.[18] In a very literal sense, then, the metaphor of substitution in reference to Christ's atonement applies for animals as well. So while animals might still be sacrificed in Jerusalem until 70 CE, within the Christian scheme of things, it is no longer necessary to sacrifice animals for the benefit of human beings. The animals might point out that within this Christian scheme there are appropriate sacrifices yet to be offered to God, which are characterized in Heb 13:15–16 as the sacrifice of good works and sharing one's goods and the sacrifice of praise emanating from lips that confess the name of the

---

17. Attridge, *Hebrews*, is rare among commentators in his rather blunt characterization of the author's critique of the efficacy of animal sacrifices. He labels it "deprecatory generalizing" (248), and sees in 9:19 a "disparaging reference" to the blood of animals and other means of purification (261). Perhaps the author should recall what Witherington, *Letters and Homilies*, 273, calls the "blood principle of Lev 17:11," that blood represents life, and blood offered up is the offering of life to God. Moreover, Northcott, *Environment*, 186, argues that sacrifice is an act of valuation of animals that involves a restoration of the created order—divine and human—in relationship and thankfulness for the goodness and giftedness of this order.

18. Johnson, *Hebrews*, 250, argues that nothing in Hebrews suggests that the letter need be dated later than the fall of the Jerusalem temple in 70 CE. In fact, the language of 10:2–3 would fit a situation in which the temple and its sacrificial offerings were still being carried out. This would provide a startling contrast for the author's argument—the perpetual sacrifices currently offered in the temple show that they are unable to attain the forgiveness of sin that is accomplished in Christ's once-for-all sacrifice.

Lord.[19] This latter sacrifice is one that the animals themselves might share in offering to God, in fulfillment of the final command of the Psalter, without the prospect of their sacrificial death looming in the background: "Let everything that breathes praise the Lord!" (Ps 150:6).[20]

In a more substantive way, though, the animals might claim a share in Christ's redemption. I argued in ch. 2 above that the implications derived from an ecological reading of Heb 1:2–3a suggest that all of creation falls within the beneficence and salvific concern of God.[21] Crucial to this insight is the observation that the Son who created and sustains the universe (1:2–3a) also took on human flesh and blood to accomplish his redemptive work (2:14). This "incarnation" provides the identification of human beings with Earth in the Son, for according to Gen 2:7, human physicality is derived from the "dust of the ground." But later in this narrative in Genesis, it is said that God created the animals "out of the ground" (v. 19). So we see an essential connection between human beings and animals (to be explored further below), and both in connection with Christ, who took on the stuff of corporeality to redeem all things connected to Earth: the human, the other than human animal, and the other than animal creation. This is the hope to which Paul alludes in Rom 8:19–21, a fulfillment of the prophetic depiction of the new heavens and new earth in which the wolf and lamb feed together and the lion eats straw like the ox (Isa 65:25).[22]

---

19. Bruce, *Hebrews*, 238, 384, notes that within Judaism, particularly at Qumran, such a view of appropriate sacrifice apart from animal sacrifice is present (1QS 9:4–5; 4QFlor 1:6; 1QH 1:28). Yet, as Bruce notes, this did not constitute a total repudiation of animal sacrifice in principle (384). Such a phenomenon is observable in Philo as well. He can extol a primarily spiritual understanding of sacrificial ritual (e.g., *Plant.* 126–35; *Spec. Laws* 1:267–72), but he can also criticize the position that literal performance of the sacrifices can be abandoned for a spiritualized application (*Migr.* 89–93). In Greek thought, several writers spoke against animal sacrifice in favor of practice of virtue as appropriate worship (e.g., Euripides, *Madness of Hercules* 1345; Philostratus, *Life of Apollonius* 1:1). Among Roman writers, Seneca articulates this position with special focus on the innocence of animal victims (*De beneficiis* 1:6:3). This view also finds a home among early Christians (e.g., *Diogn.* 3:3–5).

20. Cf. 2 *En.* 51:5, long recension.

21. Shemesh, "'And Many Beasts,'" argues that the book of Jonah affirms God's benevolence toward animals.

22. 2 *Bar.* 73:6 states that in the messianic kingdom, animals will experience transformation and be at peace and harmony with humankind (cf. 2 *En.* 58:5, short recension).

Identification of Animals with Human Beings

The criteria of ecological hermeneutics seem more naturally to address the matter of identification before proceeding to the matter of retrieval. In this instance, however, it seems that one of the significant things to which animals might wish to speak is the issue of human domination and exploitation of animals that is so vividly exemplified in the sacrificial cult. And the thrust of what animals might wish to say relates to respectful human estimation of the value of animals based on an intimate identification between human beings and other than human animals.

As just noted, animals might assert their joint participation with human beings within the scope of God's redemption in Christ. This affirms not only a joint eschatological destiny based on a common locus of being in Christ, but also affirms a common source of origin.[23] The animals might direct our attention once again to the role of the narrative of Gen 2 in this identification. Crucial are the references to God's creation of the human in v. 7 and the animals in v. 19 from the earth. While the creation of the human originates from the "dust of the ground" and the animals simply from the "ground," the verb for their creation is the same (Heb. *yāṣar*), a verb frequently used of potters shaping their vessels.[24] However, interpreters have often argued that v. 7 contains one element that clearly marks human beings as the special creation of God in contradistinction with the animals: the human possesses the "breath of life" (*nishmat hayyim*) inbreathed by God, often understood as the "spirit" or "soul." This element is missing from v. 19. However, the next three times this or similar idioms appear in Genesis, all in the flood narrative, they appear in connection with animals: *ruah hayyim* (Gen 6:17; 7:15) and *nishmat ruah hayyim* (7:22). Moreover, in Gen 2:19, when the animals are brought before the human being for naming, they are referred to as "living creatures" (*nefesh hayyah*). Though often obscured in English translations (e.g., "living soul" KJV; "living being" NRSV), the human being, upon having received the breath of life from God, is referred to with the same Hebrew phrase. To summarize, according to various biblical narratives, both human beings and other than human animals share in essence the

---

23. Of course, Eccl 3:19 affirms another connection between human beings and animals, that being the common experience of physical death.

24. The solidarity between human beings and the world, including animals, affirmed by virtue of their common creation from the dust, is found in 4 *Ezra* 7:62, 116 (cf. 5:48).

origins of their physicality, the possession of the "breath of life," and the designation "living beings," thus "completing the literary similarity between Adam and the animals."[25]

Of course, the identification of human beings with other than human animals is not an end in itself. If animals are co-recipients of redemption with human beings, and if in essence human beings and animals are intricately connected with one another, then there is an ethical consideration that must be addressed. Ethical treatment of animals, within both religious and non-religious arenas, has become a topic drawing heavy interest in recent decades.[26] The animals, by way of reminder, call human beings to ever more vigilance in addressing these matters, especially those human beings who consider seriously an ecological reading of the Bible.

An exhaustive survey of biblical-theological approaches to animal ethics is not possible here. It is interesting to note, however, that theological interest in animal ethics, though of significant interest recently, has had its advocates in earlier ages. Within Christian traditions, John Calvin found place in his exegesis and theology to portray animals as pursuing God as their true end and possessing a dignity of their own,[27] John Wesley saw animals within the scope of God's love for and redemption of the whole cosmos and thus as objects of human compassionate treatment,[28] and C. S. Lewis speculated about the eternal destiny of animals, was deeply concerned about animal pain and suffering, and famously argued against

---

25. Stone, "The Soul," 54. The entire essay explains further the similarities between human and other than human animals, the distinctiveness of human beings, and the implications for human interactions with other than human animals. Hogue, *Tangled Bank*, 14–21, draws attention to philosopher Hans Jonas's argument for the connection between human beings and other forms of organic life. Jonas labels "existential biology" the view that all living beings are connected at root by metabolic processes and the possession of some sense of purpose that manifests in caring for their own being in some way. The position emphasizes evolutionary continuity with respect to human subjectivity, which must be prefigured in earlier forms. The net result of this "existential biology" is that it makes human beings part of nature's web of life.

26. The pioneering work of Andrew Linzey is worthy of note. Among his voluminous output in this area is his book, *Animal Gospel*, which provides, in the words of the title of his introduction, "a Christian credo for animals" (1) aimed at providing the contours of a Christian response to the suffering of innocent creatures.

27. Huff, "Calvin and the Beasts," 67–75. Huff notes that Calvin did not speculate on the eschatological redemption of animals (75).

28. Lodahl, *God of Nature*, 195–202.

the practice of vivisection.[29] So interest in animal ethics from within the framework of Christianity is no recent fad.

By way of a constructive proposal, perhaps the best that can be proffered in the present space is a general approach to an ethic toward animals that acknowledges the complexity of interactions between human beings and other than human animals that pays due attention to the uniqueness of human beings as they exist in community with the rest of the animal kingdom. Michael Hogue suggests that such a relationship must acknowledge the "tangled bank," to borrow a metaphor from Charles Darwin, and recognize that the solutions to problems of animal ethics are not likely to emerge from a tidy ecotheological ethical system, but rather a dialogical process that reflects the "untidiness of the present human relation to the natural world"[30] that keeps in view a theological vision of human participation within the divine ordering of creation.[31] Hogue's proposal is short on specific suggestions. However, Richard Wade offers what might be a way forward with what he terms a natural law ethic towards animals. Following the Roman jurist Ulpian and Thomas Aquinas, Wade argues for an application of natural law as a "duty to do what is ethically right with respect to the nature of the animal (the kind of being the animal is)" while at the same time assenting to "duties to human persons with a reasonable need."[32] Wade seeks to avoid the radical egalitarianism between human and other than human animals advanced by Peter Singer's animal liberationism while arguing for a robust Christian ethics of animals grounded in the connection between human beings and other than human animals observable in natural law.[33] Common to both Hogue and Wade is the insistence that human beings and animals are co-participants in God's creative project in the world.

In the final analysis, the voice of the animals might simply say that the identification between themselves and human beings uncovered by the paradigmatic transformation of Christ's sacrifice demands that human beings, given their unique gifts and capacities among God's creatures, use those gifts and capacities to forge an ethic toward animals that

---

29. Linzey, "C. S. Lewis' Theology of Animals," 60–81.
30. Hogue, *Tangled Bank*, 235.
31. Ibid., 244.
32. Wade, "Ethics of Animals," 205.
33. Ibid., 212. For a statement of Singer's position, see *Animal Liberation*.

recognizes their intrinsic dignity and place as cohabitants in God's world. Perhaps such a response might spur human interpreters of the Bible to rehabilitate the ambivalent view of animals found so frequently in the pages of the Bible.[34]

CONCLUSION

This study has attempted to demonstrate that the author of Hebrews has continued in the pattern of an ambivalent view of the value of other than human animals through a christocentrically and anthropocentrically biased critique of the sacrificial cult in Heb 9:11—10:18. However, we have also sought to demonstrate that the author, almost assuredly unconsciously, has provided for the possibility of an ecological reading of the passage that allows for the voice of the animals to call prophetically to human beings to view other than human animals through the transformative lens of Christ's sacrifice. The result is a reassessment of human relationships with and treatment of the animal world.

Perhaps the best way to conclude this discussion is with the confession of Andrew Linzey in his book *Animal Gospel*. Its eloquent wording captures poignantly that which this chapter has struggled to say.

> I affirm the One Creator God from whom all existence flows. I celebrate the common origin of all life in God. I undertake to cherish and love all creatures whose life belongs to God and exists for God's glory.
>
> I affirm the life of Jesus as the true pattern of service to the weak. I promise my solidarity with all suffering creatures. I join hands with Jesus in his ministry to the least of all, knowing that it is the vocation of the strong to be gentle.
>
> I see in the face of the Crucified the faces of all innocent, suffering creatures. I hear their cries for a new creation. I thank God for the grace to feel their suffering and give voice to their pain.
>
> I affirm the Word made flesh as the new covenant between God and all sentient creatures. I seek to live out that covenant in acts of moral generosity, kindness and gentleness to all those creatures that God has gathered together into unity.

---

34. Hobgood-Oster, *Friends We Keep*, argues for a reclamation of Christian tradition that has valued the place of animals in the world. She argues that the gospel may again be good news for animals that have walked with Christians throughout the ages as companions, givers of hospitality and comfort, and as fellow sufferers in the Roman arenas.

I affirm the life-giving Spirit, source of all that is wonderful, who animates every creature. I pledge myself to honor life because of the Lord of life.

I affirm the hope of the world to come for all God's creatures. I believe in the Cross as the symbol of liberation for every creature suffering from bondage. I will daily trust in the redeeming power of God to transform the universe.

I pray that the community of Christ may be blessed with a new vision of God's creation. I will turn away from my hardness of heart and seek to become a living sign of the Gospel for which all creatures long.

I rejoice in animals as fellow-creatures: loved by the Father, redeemed by the Son, and enlivened by the Holy Spirit.

May God the Holy Trinity give me strength to live out my commitment this day.[35]

---

35. Linzey, *Animal Gospel*, 7–8.

4

The Promise of God's Rest (Hebrews 4:1–11)

Joshua, Jesus, Sabbath, and the Care of the Land

INTRODUCTION

HEBREWS 4:1–11 CONTINUES THE rhetorical strategy of the letter-sermon by asserting the superiority of the Son to another key figure of the old covenant, Joshua. Specifically, the author asserts that the Israelites of Joshua's day failed to enter God's rest because of their disobedience, so that the promise of rest ostensibly given in terms of the land ultimately lay unfulfilled. The author contends that in the Son, the promise of entering God's rest remains open to the present day, and that this rest is superior to that available through Joshua because it is connected with the Sabbath rest enjoyed by God since the conclusion of the works of creation.

What the author of Hebrews has effectively done is both to spiritualize and eschatologize the promise of Joshua's rest embodied in the land such that in Jesus the promise of rest is currently realized, to be realized in full in the eschaton. This is in keeping with the author's anthropological and christological agendas throughout the letter-sermon.

However, the voice of Earth, in this context specifically the land, is heard through one of the scriptural citations proffered by the author in support of his argument (v. 4). The appeal to the establishment of Sabbath at the end of God's creative work in Gen 2:2–3 allows for the voice of the land to assert for itself a place in the enjoyment of God's rest, both in the present and in the eschaton. The land will appeal to traditions in the Hebrew Bible that demonstrate God's concern for the land in terms of Sabbath observance. The resulting reading will be one that tempers the rhetorical concerns of the author, in which a denigration of the actual land is implied, with a call to expand the scope of God's promised rest to include all creation. To this end, the principles articulated by the Consultation on Ecological Hermeneutics in the Society of Biblical Literature—suspicion, identification, retrieval—will provide the shape of this discussion.

REINTERPRETING THE PROMISE OF THE LAND

Various biases against the land are evident in this instance of the author's rhetorical strategy of comparing old covenantal images to the Son. The point of departure for these biases is the statement in 4:8: "For if Joshua had given them rest, God would not speak later about another day." The ostensible promise of God that the land of Canaan would be the place in which the promised rest would be fulfilled is relativized by the author of Hebrews. At this point, history is on the side of our author—rarely in Israel's history is there an extended sense of rest in the land. But more to the point in the present argument is that the prospect for genuine fulfillment of the promise through the entry of the people under Joshua into Canaan was virtually doomed from the start: the original recipients of the promise died in the desert because of their lack of faithfulness. Nevertheless, another generation did eventually enter the land, in what would appear to be the fulfillment of the promise to receive a land flowing with milk and honey. However, here the author of Hebrews, through a creative exegesis of biblical texts, argues that in fact Joshua's entry into Canaan was, at best, but a precursor to the genuine fulfillment of the promise of rest in the Son. At worst, Joshua's conquest might be considered a distraction to the genuine fulfillment of the promised rest. So in Heb 4:1–11 we find the author's corrective reinterpretation of the promise in terms of its fulfillment in the Son, put forth in support of the author's overarching interest of demonstrating the superiority of the Son to the old covenant.

So how has the author of Hebrews reinterpreted the promise of the land? This is a question that has concerned traditional exegesis of the passage for centuries. A significant component of this reinterpretation is a restriction of focus. It is clear from a reading of portions of Exodus, Leviticus, and Deuteronomy, that connected with the actual reception of the land was a covenantal framework that instructed the Israelites how they must interact with and treat the land on which they would live. We will have more to say on this below, but for the present, it is noteworthy that the author of Hebrews has restricted consideration of the land to the possession of the land only. Given the parameters and rhetorical strategy of the letter-sermon's argumentation, this is an understandable move. This restriction of focus leads naturally into the framing of the issue in this manner: did Israel's entrance into the promised land of Canaan produce the rest promised them by God? For our author, this leads to the answer, "No." Then how will God fulfill this promise? In the Son. So in the first instance, we detect a bias against the land as an entity of integrity and inherent value through the restriction of its place in this argument as the prize won that ultimately did not rise to the level of fulfillment of its promise. This exemplifies what we have argued earlier, namely, that the author's bias is primarily christological, aimed at establishing the supremacy of the Son in the comparison of covenants, with the derivative anthropological benefits that flow from this christological emphasis.[1]

Another way in which bias against the land is evident occurs through what might be called the "spiritualization" of the promise of the land. This phenomenon occurs again in Hebrews with respect to the land in 11:8–16 and 12:22–27. The emphasis in each of these passages falls on a reinterpretation of the promise of the land that denies any place to the literal fulfillment of the promise in terms of geography. While it is fairly clear in 11:8–16 and 12:22–27 that the spiritual reinterpretation is achieved largely through framing the fulfillment of the promise eschatologically, it is not so clear whether the fulfillment of promise in 4:1–11 occurs in the present experience of believers or in the future. Commentators are divided on this matter. Typical of those who argue for an eschatological referent is Johnson, who points out that the author defines as the ultimate fulfillment of the promise the attainment of glory for human beings (2:10), which is an eschatological blessing, with the present life characterized as a pilgrimage of moral and spiritual dedication toward this goal (4:11).[2] Further exegetical warrant is found in the characterization of rest as ces-

---

1. See ch. 2 above.

2. Johnson, *Hebrews*, 130–31; Koester, *Hebrews*, 270, 279; Ellingworth, *Hebrews*, 246; Attridge, *Hebrews*, 131; O'Brien, *Hebrews*, 160, 164–66. Bruce, *Hebrews*, 110, appears to fall into this camp: "It is evidently an experience which they do not enjoy in their present mortal life, although it belongs to them as a heritage, and by faith they may live in the good of it here and now."

sation from labor in v. 10, a reality for believers that apparently lay in the future. Those who depict the promised rest as a present reality for believers do not deny an ultimate eschatological fulfillment, but depict God's rest as participation in God's life through faith and cessation from dead works, at least to the degree that the experience of salvation is available in the present.[3] The present tense verbs in vv. 3, 6, 9 and the frequent refrain of the word "today" in this passage (v. 7) and the preceding context (3:7, 13, 15) further buttress this position.[4] Resolution of this problem is not immediately germane to the present discussion. What is germane is what the two positions share in common: the spiritualization of the promise of the land. The land is not addressed in its own right as such; it is reconceptualized christologically and packaged as a blessing for those who remain faithful and obedient. In this respect, Heb 4:1–11 is part of a trajectory of NT thought that collapsed an etherealized and detached sense of sacred space—primarily the temple and land—into the people of God (e.g., Eph 2:21–22; 1 Pet 2:5).[5]

The two biases identified to this point—restriction of focus and spiritualization of the promise—originate in the argumentation of the author of Hebrews, though the nature of the latter bias is variously understood by subsequent commentators. There is a third bias that might be identified at this point, a minority position that manifests in two ways. This bias interestingly envisions a literal fulfillment to the promise of the land. In its more scholarly presentation, Buchanan argues that spiritualized interpretations of the promise betray the theological interests of commentators more than the intent of the author of Hebrews. Buchanan's understanding of the passage sees the argumentation of Hebrews as following a historically linear progression. The promise of the land that was available to the Isrealites in Joshua's day and is reaffirmed as open in David's day, evident in the author's use of traditions from Num 14 and Ps 95, is currently available to the author's contemporaries in the

3. Witherington, *Letters and Homilies*, 177, 182; Lane, *Hebrews 1–8*, 99; Craddock, *Hebrews*, 52; Jewett, *Letter to Pilgrims*, 66–67; Schenck, *Cosmology and Eschatology*, 60–63.

4. Lane, *Hebrews 1–8*, 99, argues that the author's separation of God's rest from God's creative work in his appropriation of Gen 2:2 (v. 4) demonstrates that the rest is not part of creation. Were it part of creation, Lane argues, it would give rise to the notion that God had prepared a place of rest as part of the created order to be revealed in the future. The separation of rest from creation eliminates this possibility in Lane's estimation.

5. Northcott, *Environment*, 108.

Son.[6] While Buchanan's view has not garnered much scholarly support,[7] it does indicate that a reading other than a spiritualized one is possible. On a more popular level, a literal fulfillment of the promise of the land is prominent in the various dispensationalist systems of the likes of Hal Lindsey, John Hagee, and Tim LaHaye. Here the restoration of Jews to the land promised to Abraham and initially realized in Joshua's conquest is a precursor to the parousia of Christ. While at first glance these positions appear to be an advance upon the spiritualized promise of the land, they suffer from the first of the biases noted in the author. Both Buchanan's and the dispensationalist views, while seeing the promise of the land as a literal, concrete possession of the land, do so only in the restrictive terms of the author of Hebrews. Buchanan's assessment largely advances a political reality: the reacquisition of the land as constitutive of ethnic identity. Dispensationalist views do the same, with the practical payoff the political, economic, and military support of the present state of Israel, with an eye toward how this plays itself out eschatologically. In neither Buchanan's nor dispensationalist views is the land viewed in its own right, but only as it serves other anthropologically determined ends.

The criterion of suspicion has led us to discover several areas of bias against the land as an entity in its own right. The wellbeing of the land is simply ignored in our author's discussion. The land is an object of comparison only in terms of its possession and ability to produce the benefit of rest for the people. The conclusions drawn by the author of Hebrews deny the land's ability to provide for the people that which was ostensibly promised through the possession of the land, while at the same time concluding that the land in and of itself is of no importance for experiencing the benefits of the new covenant. The reception of the blessing of God's rest, once connected to possession of the land, has been severed from the land and relocated in the Son. And even those theological constructions that hold to the importance of the land do so at the expense of any consideration of wellbeing for the land. But this is not the final word on the

---

6. Buchanan, *Hebrews*, 72–74.

7. A large number of commentaries either mention Buchanan's position, sometimes characterizing it as idiosyncratic, or do not mention it at all. Ellingworth, *Hebrews*, 254, while rejecting this position, does applaud Buchanan's caution against a too hastily drawn conclusion that a heaven/earth dualism is determinative here. Cadwallader, "Earth as Host," 149–50, draws on Buchanan's scheme to identify the exigence behind the discussion of Heb 11 in his own ecological reading of that passage.

matter, for the author of Hebrews has seeded our passage, albeit probably unconsciously, with some means by which we might identify with the land and thus recover soundings of its voice.

RE-ESTABLISHING A CONNECTION WITH THE LAND

Before examining how the notion of Sabbath might provide a connection with the land, we need to examine briefly how the author of Hebrews employs the notion of the Sabbath in the argumentation of Heb 4:1–11. The discussion of ch. 4 proceeds on the heels of an exegesis of Ps 95 [94 LXX]:7–11 in Heb 3:7–19. The author has cited the psalm to accomplish two purposes. First, it demonstrates the failure of the wilderness generation to enter God's rest due to their disobedience and faithlessness, a crucial component for the following paranaesis. But second, the collocation of the word "today" (*sēmeron*, Ps 95:7) with the noun "rest" (*katapausis*, v. 11) allows the author to argue that despite the failure of the generations of Joshua and David to enter God's rest, there remains an availability of this rest for the believers of the author's day.[8] But the author has one more move to make in the passage. Through the use of *gezera shawa*, an interpretive technique that links passages together on the basis of common vocabulary, the author redefines that which constitutes the rest of which he speaks. Genesis 2:2 is cited in Heb 4:4, with the verb "rest" (*katapauō*) connected to the cognate noun from Ps 95:11[9] in a move that allows the author to transfer the idea of rest from "a land for Israel to a condition of participation in God."[10] The conclusion drawn from this exegesis is found in v. 9, where with a term unique to the Greek Bible, *sabbitismos*, the author affirms that there is a "Sabbath rest" available through the Son for those who remain faithful and obedient, and that this Sabbath rest is nothing short of participation in the divine life.[11] The creative interpretation of Ps 95:7, 11 with Gen 2:2 within the rhetorical strategy of favorably comparing the Son to aspects of the old covenant produces a reading that

---

8. Johnson, *Hebrews*, 128; Lane, *Hebrews* 1–8, 100–1, who sees "today" as indicating a prophetically announced time when the rest would be made available to God's people.

9. Bruce, *Hebrews*, 106, points out that two different Hebrew words for "rest" lay behind the Greek *katapau-* cognates in Ps 95:11 and Gen 2:2 (*měnûḥâ* and *šābat*, respectively). The author's reliance on the LXX here is crucial for making his point.

10. Craddock, *Hebrews*, 52.

11. Johnson, *Hebrews*, 129.

effectively removes the significance of the land from consideration of the promise of rest.

Given how thoroughly the author has stripped the actual land of any significance through the use of Sabbath, how might we use Sabbath as a point of identification with the land? In essence, we will do as the author of Hebrews did. We will connect his use of Sabbath in Heb 4 with other passages in order to reintroduce a consideration of the land in its own right.

Habel has studied the images employed in the Hebrew Bible to depict the land in terms of its relationships with God and the people who live on the land as well as the exercise of power in the use of the land.[12] Of the six images discussed, the one most pertinent for our purposes is the agrarian ideology described in Lev 25–27.[13] This understanding of the land depicts the land as God's own personal sanctuary and garden, worked by Israelite families who live on their traditional properties as tenant farmers (Lev 25:23). The land belongs to God and is granted in trust to the Israelites. And the land is to be operated within the framework of a Sabbath economy.

An illustrative text for our purposes of identification with the land through Sabbath is Exod 23:10–12:

> For six years you shall sow your land and gather in its yield; but the seventh year you shall let it rest and lie fallow, so that the poor of your people may eat; and what they leave the wild animals may eat. You shall do the same with your vineyard, and with your olive orchard. Six days you shall do your work, but on the seventh day you shall rest, so that your ox and your donkey may have relief, and your homeborn slave and the resident alien may be refreshed.

Two points are significant here. First, note that the land itself is to experience the benefits of Sabbath rest. It may be worked for six years, but on the seventh it is to lie fallow. Second, the land's experience of Sabbath rest is brought into connection with the Sabbath rest experienced by the Israelites. In the same way that the Israelites work six days and rest the seventh, so too is the land worked for six years and rested the seventh. Moreover, in the fiftieth year, the Year of Jubilee, not only is land that

---

12. Habel, *Land*. Hillel, *Natural History*, offers another understanding of how these images developed.

13. Habel, *Land*, ch. 6.

had been lost restored to its original owner (Lev 25:10)—an indication of the tenant status of the Israelites on the land—but the land is again to lie fallow. An experience of human liberation is coupled with rest once again for the land.[14]

This connection of the land with its inhabitants through mutual experience of Sabbath rest is further cemented in Lev 26:3–45 in terms of the relationship between human faithfulness and obedience to the commands of God and the fruitfulness of the land.[15] In vv. 3–13, God promises to bless the people with rains and agricultural productivity if only the people would follow in the statutes given them by God. This harkens back to 25:18–22, where God explains that it will be through God's blessings that the people, as they practice the Sabbath year rest for the land, will eat for three years on what is planted in the sixth year. If the people follow all of God's statutes, including the Sabbath year rest for the land, they will dwell securely in a land that will produce crops for them in abundance.

But with Lev 26:14–45 the flipside reality is described in shocking detail. If the people do not obey the statutes of God, then the land will not produce for the people, and should disobedience persist, God will eventually uproot the people from the land promised them. It is in this ultimate expression of God's fury that we see a significant relationship between human behavior and the land:

> Then the land shall enjoy its sabbath years as long as it lies desolate, while you are in the land of your enemies; then the land shall rest, and enjoy its sabbath years. As long as it lies desolate, it shall have the rest it did not have on your sabbaths when you were living on it. (Lev 26:34–35)

The expulsion of the disobedient from the land will give the land its due Sabbath rest. This is probably best understood in two senses. First, human sinfulness itself is disruptive to the wellbeing of the land, for it disrupts the covenantal framework for holistic life for the people upon entrance into the land of promise. Second, it is probable that in the extreme disobedience that brought about exile, among the statutes of God ignored were the commands to allow the land its Sabbath rest. At any rate, God's personal sanctuary and garden is polluted by human sinfulness and

---

14. For a more fully developed argument see Richter, "Environmental Law," 355–76.
15. Cf. Deut 28:1–24; 29:22–29; Lev 18:24–28.

short of repentance it is only through expulsion of the perpetrators that the wellbeing of the land is restored.

Another of the images of the land described by Habel is instructive here: the prophetic ideology.[16] In this image the land is depicted as God's pure and precious heritage, and the land suffers great anguish when defiled by the people God has planted in the land. The situation envisioned in Lev 26:33—the exile of the people from the land due to their sinfulness—has come to pass and has received critique in the words of the prophets (e.g., Isa 7:23–25; 8:21–22; 9:18–21; 24:4–6; 32:9–14; 33:7–9; 34:8–17; Jer 4:23–26; Amos 4:7–9). The land suffers from human sinfulness and injustice. It is interesting that in the prophetic critiques the land is depicted as enduring great agony because of the sins of the people, while in Lev 26:34–35 the land is seen as experiencing its long denied Sabbaths. From both perspectives, however, the fact that the human inhabitants did not act rightly in terms of their relationship with God and the land has brought about a state of affairs that has fallen far short of the intended ideal.

What we have seen to this point is that the Sabbath is a point of contact between the people of God and the land. Sabbath establishes a context for human care for the land, and human righteousness and sinfulness have consequences for the land. Sabbath illustrates the connectedness of all relations between humans, the land, and God.[17] We will develop in the final section of this chapter the significance of this identification for retrieving the voice of the land, but before then we must examine one more aspect of human identification with the land: the place of the Son.

The author of Hebrews is adamant that the Sabbath rest of God is available to the people of God in the person of the Son. In Lev 26:40–45, God specifies that exile is not the last word for the people or for the land. In particular, v. 42 states that once the people have repented of their wickedness, God would remember both the people and the land. Having had its Sabbath rest, the desolate land would be reunited with its repentant tenants. In Second Isaiah, this reunion finds expression in a series of five sections in which the renewal of the physical world is preceded by the appearance of a servant figure: 41:8–20; 42:1–13; 49:1–13; 50:4—51:3;

---

16. Habel, *Land*, ch. 5.
17. Northcott, *Environment*, 190.

52:13—55:13.[18] This figure acts humbly and compassionately for the benefit of others, and one result of this beneficent action is the transformation of the physical order. Early on in Christian circles this servant of Second Isaiah became identified with Jesus Christ. If such an identification lay in the back of our author's mind, then this may suggest that in the author's claim that the Sabbath rest of God is found in the Son, the land is also included within the purview of this rest. This is an identification of indirection. In the Son is God's Sabbath rest. Using a similar strategy to that of the author of Hebrews, we have seen that we might reconnect his new understanding of Sabbath with earlier biblical depictions of Sabbath that connect human beings and their actions to the land. If the interconnected destinies of the people and the land involve blessing, cursing, and finally redemption, all describable within the framework of Sabbath, then the Son's role in bringing about a reality of the human experience of God's Sabbath rest might plausibly entail a similar experience for the land. So in the joint foci of Sabbath and Son, the author of Hebrews has provided the constructs through which human beings might identify with the land, all, of course, outside of his intent. With this connection established, we now turn to the task of hearing the voice of the land in Heb 4:1–11.

RETRIEVING THE VOICE OF THE LAND

The starting point for hearing the voice of the land in Heb 4:1–11 must be an understanding that there is some sense in which the promised rest is available in the present. If the promised rest is strictly a future reality, then the voice of the land asserts, at best, a claim that there is a future redemption for the land as well. And while we would not deny an eschatological redemption for the whole of creation, certainly there is more to hear from the land than this. But as we noted earlier, many of those who argue for a present experience of God's Sabbath rest do so in a spiritualized sense that has specifically anthropocentric benefits in view. Here Jewett moves us forward in our understanding of the significance of experiencing God's rest in the present. The rest of God is not the attainment of some

---

18. See Grey, "'Trees of the Field.'" Brown, *Seven Pillars of Creation*, 200–1, notes that the metaphor of "stretching out" in Second Isaiah shows God "stretching out" the heavens in connection with establishing the Earth (cf. 44:24; 45:12; 48:13; 51:13) as an act of creation. Similarly, God commands Zion to "stretch out" her habitations after her desolation (54:1–3), depicting the re-establishment of Zion in terms of an act of re-creation.

predetermined eschatologically experienced goal or virtue, but is rather "to be encountered by Christ, who addresses us in the kerygma, and in responding by faith, to carry on the enlivening dialogue."[19] Participation in this "enlivening dialogue" then "inserts dynamic activism into what has traditionally been a passive concept."[20] Crucial here is a proper understanding of what is meant by the phrase "God's rest." Clearly rest cannot equal inactivity, for both God and the Son are depicting in Hebrews as being active in the affairs of the world (e.g., 1:3; 7:25).[21] Rather, God's rest is equivalent in meaning to "God's own way of existing,"[22] with believers' experience of God's rest as participation in the divine life.[23] The present experience of God's rest, then, is not the passive reception of spiritual blessings, much less the passive waiting for their eschatological reception, but is rather an ongoing conversation with the Son as to how we might more actively participate in the divine life for the benefit of the world. So the first thing the land might say to us is to focus on God's rest as a present reality for believers that carries with it the challenge to engage the Son in dialogue to hear how we might work to bring the call of the Gospel into action in the world.

A second way in which the land might speak to us is to remind us that the principle of *gezerah shawa* works both ways. Recall that this formed one of the bases upon which we built an identification between human beings and the land. If the author of Hebrews is justified in reinterpreting the promise of the land through linking the term "rest" in Ps 95:11 and Gen 2:2, then we should see what happens when we link the term "Sabbath" in Heb 4:1–11 and passages from the Hebrew Bible in which the word occurs. We saw that what resulted was a profound relationship between human beings, the land, and God under the rubric of Sabbath, an interconnectedness that finds fresh expression in the person of the Son. So rather than providing the basis for a denigration of the land, the Son as the full expression of God's rest actually provides the grounds for a reinvigorated, robust performance of the care of the land in the spirit of

---

19. Jewett, *Letter*, 67.
20. Ibid., 67.
21. So Koester, *Hebrews*, 279.
22. Johnson, *Hebrews*, 125.
23. Ibid., 129; Craddock, *Hebrews*, 52.

those outlined in the various Sabbath regulations of Torah.[24] If anything, the connection of human beings with the land has been taken up in the Son, and as such, demands a more conscientious response from human beings than even under the old covenant. So the land might say to us, on the model and in the authority of the Son, "You have heard it said of old that you should give me, the land, its Sabbath rest, but I say to you, show me the care worthy of a fellow recipient of the promise of God's Sabbath rest."

A third way in which the land might speak to us is by pointing us directly to Gen 2:2 as the author of Hebrews did in 4:2 and 10. On the seventh day God is said to have rested from the works God had done. But the land might also have us read Gen 2:3, which speaks of God blessing and sanctifying the seventh day because God rested from God's creative work. Here we are reminded that God's Sabbath rest is hallowed and holy precisely in connection with God's creative work. The author's use of Gen 2:2 apart from v. 3 indicates the desire of the author to separate God's work of creation from God's subsequent rest in order to establish that the Sabbath rest is itself a primordial reality that stands open for believers from the conclusion of God's creative work to the present day.[25] This separation of v. 2 from v. 3 reflects another of the author's biases in favor of human benefit over against consideration of the land. What the land argues in response is that one must consider the context in which God's Sabbath rest is deemed blessed and holy. And that context is provided in Gen 2:3, omitted by the author of Hebrews. Consideration of what this verse contributes to our understanding of God's Sabbath rest leads to the land's word to us on this head: the Creator's rest is an affirmation of the cosmos as good, blessed, and enjoyed by the Creator.[26] And as such, consideration for the land is part and parcel of the present experience of God's Sabbath rest.[27]

24. Richter, "Environmental Law," surveys the issue of care of the land in the Torah, particularly in Deuteronomy. She sees Deuteronomy as the *politeia* of ancient Israel and examines care of the land in this structure in terms of the following categories: the land and its produce; the produce and the poor; the land and agriculture; the land and warfare; and the creatures of the land. She concludes that according to Torah, economic security, national security, and family economic viability provide no excuse for environmental abuse, even in view of short-term urgency.

25. Lane, *Hebrews 1–8*, 99.

26. Northcott, *Environment*, 188. See also Moltmann, *God in Creation*, 277–78.

27. J. Laansma, "Hidden Stories," 9–18, argues for a structure of Hebrews as follows: 1:1—4:13 speaks of sonship and the cosmos, while 4:14—10:25 speaks of High Priest and

Perhaps the final word the land might speak to us is to point us again back to Gen 2, much in the same way that the author of Hebrews did in crafting his argument. But instead of going to v. 2, the land points us to v. 15:

> "Then Yahweh Elohim took the human and put him into the garden of Eden to tend it (*lĕʾobdāh*) and protect it (*lĕšomrāh*)."[28]

The land, which is frequently depicted as the garden, sanctuary, and heritage of God, has been placed under the protective care of human beings. Notwithstanding the tension created between this verse and Gen 1:26, which is frequently cited as a text sanctioning the human exploitation of creation,[29] Gen 2:15 functions as the connective tissue between the statement that God rested after finishing the works of creation (v. 2) and the subsequent Pentateuchal legislation concerning the care of the land. And despite the interjection of human sin into the narrative of Gen 3, there is no indication that the mandate given to human beings to care for the garden has been abrogated. So in reminding human beings of Gen 2:15, the land is telling human beings not only to read Gen 2:2, as the author of Hebrews had us read, but to keep on reading to discover something about what it is that makes us human.

There is much the land has had us consider once we uncovered its voice. Some might accuse us of creating a conversation that is simply not present in Heb 4:1–11. I prefer to think of it as deducing implications of what the author might have said on these matters were they his primary rhetorical concern, given what he has written in the passage. Using cues from the passage itself, and borrowing some of the author's exegetical toolkit, we utilized the principles of ecological hermeneutics to explore what the land might say to us in light of Heb 4:1–11. We do not deny the

---

the earthly/heavenly tabernacles. In 3:7—4:13, the transition from the first to the second section, the focus is on the "rest" of God via appeal to Ps 95. According to Laansma, what this accomplishes is a linkage between cosmos and sanctuary through the concept of Sabbath rest that draws upon the Ancient Near Eastern and OT tendency to connect cosmos and sanctuary. The net effect is that "the construct assumed in Hebrews' imagery and argument is precisely that creation is being reclaimed as God's temple" (14). For our purposes, the importance is that by virtue of the introduction of the notion of Sabbath rest, the land is granted significance in the redemptive purposes of God. For further discussion on this motif, see Beale, *Temple*, 29–167; and Walton, *Ancient Near Eastern Thought*, 113–34.

28. Translation from Richter, "Environmental Law," 376.
29. Cain, *Ecological Theology*, ch. 4.

concerns of the author, nor do we deny the substance of the argument. We just wish to expand the scope of discussion to hear the concerns of Earth.

CONCLUSION

This study does not pretend to be an exhaustive exegetical treatment of Heb 4:1–11. It has sought only to uncover the voice of the land that has been subsumed under the rhetorical and theological interests of the author of Hebrews. In this task, the criteria of ecological hermeneutics have assisted us. The criterion of suspicion uncovered several areas of bias, some by the author of Hebrews and others by subsequent commentators, that have in common the denigration of the land by eliminating from consideration those aspects of interaction with the land that come with its possession and by eliminating the significance of the very land itself in favor of the Son. We saw that even those fringe positions that hold out some significance for the literal fulfillment of the promise of the land did not advance beyond anthropocentrically derived calculations of the benefit of the land for human beings. The criterion of identification drew our attention to the author's emphasis on the concept of the Sabbath as a means by which human beings might identify with the land. By way of Sabbath, human beings rediscover the Hebrew Bible's emphasis on the close connection between human activity and behavior and the wellbeing of the land, a connection at the heart of various prophetic critiques of the abuse of the land that results from human sin and injustice. The criterion of retrieval led us to hear the land's call to live out our identification with the land and so expand our understanding of the promise of God's rest to include the land, and indeed, the whole of creation.

In the final analysis, this reading of Heb 4:1–11 need not be construed in such a way as to deny wholesale the focus and rhetorical strategy of the author. Rather, it is simply an attempt to pick up on clues in the text itself, draw in other canonical voices, and hear the plaintive voice of the land through these cues. Suspicion need not equal rejection; it may but serve as a call to dig beneath the surface of the text to find those voices that linger just below our notice in order to give them a hearing. It is my hope that this study has done just that for the land in Heb 4:1–11.

5

A Whispered Voice in the Choir

Toward an Ecological Pneumatology in Hebrews

INTRODUCTION

THE LETTER-SERMON OF HEBREWS is rich in language about God and the Son, but language about the Holy Spirit is remarkably less well represented. There are five clear references to the Holy Spirit (2:4; 3:7; 6:4; 9:8; and 10:15), with two other likely references (9:14; 10:29). Such paucity is explicable in light of the author's rhetorical purposes, namely, to discuss what God has done to effect the new covenant through the Son. In this rhetoric, the role of the Holy Spirit is largely confirmatory of that which the Son has accomplished in the drama of redemption. In this respect, the view of the Holy Spirit adopted by the author of Hebrews is what Jürgen Moltmann has labeled the "Spirit of Christ," a view that emphasizes what Christ has done to procure and effect salvation for human beings. As such, another view of the Holy Spirit identified by Moltmann, the "Spirit of God," is undeveloped in Hebrews. It is this view that emphasizes the role of the Spirit in God's work as Creator.

This study will examine the references to the Holy Spirit in Hebrews to see if there are any grounds for asserting a place for an emphasis on the "Spirit of God" in the few references made, even while granting the author's preference for the "Spirit of Christ" emphasis. The discussion will argue that one text in particular, 9:14, provides a context for doing so. The pneumatology of Moltmann will serve as a framework for identifying such an emphasis in these references, thus providing the foundation for an ecological component to the sketchy pneumatology of Hebrews. If

Hebrews is a vocal piece in which the dominant voices in the choir sing of christology and soteriology as they benefit human beings, the Spirit is cast as a small, even whispered voice that provides minor harmonies to the dominant strains.

Again, the principles of ecological hermeneutics developed by the Consultation on Ecological Hermeneutics Section in the Society of Biblical Literature—suspicion, identification, retrieval—will form the shape of this study.

SUSPICION:
THE WHISPERED VOICE IN THE CHOIR

As noted, Hebrews contains very few references to the Holy Spirit. For the most part, those few references are themselves rather sparse in terms of substantial content about the nature and work of the Holy Spirit in the redemptive drama described in the author's argumentation.[1] At the outset, we might say that the Holy Spirit's place in the rhetoric of Hebrews is largely a supporting role to the place of the Son in the rhetoric. We will examine each of these passages in turn.

The first mention of the Spirit is found in 2:4. The immediate context, begun in v. 3, is the proclamation of the salvation that was declared by the Lord, understood here as the Son, that was further attested to the author's circle by those who heard the Lord, and that was further confirmed by God through the added testimony of signs, wonders, miracles, and "by gifts of the Holy Spirit, distributed according to his will." The NRSV obscures a syntactical issue in the Greek with its translation that understands the "gifts" to be that which is distributed according to the Spirit's will, in agreement with 1 Cor 12:11.[2] However, a more natural reading is that the Spirit is itself that which is distributed by God in joint testimony of the veracity of the proclamation of salvation.[3] Precise resolution of the syntactical issue is not significant for our purposes; what is significant is

---

1. Allen, "'Forgotten Spirit,'" 51–66, argues that though the number of actual references to the Spirit is sparse in Hebrews, a few strategic references actually form a significant piece of the evidence that the readers are indeed participants in the new covenant.

2. Johnson, *Hebrews*, 89; Lane, *Hebrews 1-8*, 41; and O'Brien, *Hebrews*, 90, are sympathetic toward this understanding. For a discussion of the syntactical issues, see Ellingworth, *Hebrews*, 142.

3. Attridge, *Hebrews*, 67–68; Bruce, *Hebrews*, 69; Buchanan, *Hebrews*, 26–27; Koester, *Hebrews*, 211.

the function of the Holy Spirit in the statement of our author. Whether the gifts of the Spirit or the Spirit itself, the function of the Spirit is in confirmation of the apostolic proclamation of the salvation declared by the Lord. In other words, the Spirit performs a subordinate role in support of the author's primary rhetorical concern, which is to draw attention to "so great a salvation" as that provided in the Son (Heb 2:3).

The next reference is found in 3:7. Here the Holy Spirit is introduced as the one who speaks through a biblical quotation from Ps 95.[4] The shift in subjects between God and the Holy Spirit as the author of Scripture is a relatively common occurrence among ancient exegetes, both Christian (cf. Acts 28:25; 1 *Clem.* 13:1; 16:2) and Jewish (e.g., *m. Soṭah* 9:6).[5] But the issue here is not precisely the authority behind an ancient text, but rather the present application of this text to the community by virtue of its contemporary reappropriation in direct revelation through the Holy Spirit. This is especially remarkable in light of the author's earlier comments arguing that the revelation of the Son surpassed the old revelation of the prophets, which included the words of Scripture (Heb 1:1).[6] Here, however, Scripture is made efficacious, living, and powerful through the present voice of the Holy Spirit. Commentators frequently draw attention to the present tense of the verb "says," the refrain throughout the passage, "today, if you hear his voice," and the author's interpretation of the word "today" (3:7, 13, 15; 4:7). The point of the reference seems to be that the same Spirit who brought the community to faith initially (cf. 2:4) continues to speak to them in their present circumstances through the words of the quoted psalm.[7] The net effect for our purposes is that the Spirit speaks to draw attention to the author's call for the community to enter into the Sabbath rest provided in the Son (4:1–11).[8] A similar sense is found in the reference to the Holy Spirit in 10:15, though the biblical text in which the Spirit speaks (Jer 31:33–34) and the specific application (the superiority of the new covenant) are, of course, different.[9] The focus in both 3:7 and

---

4. For a discussion on the use of Scripture in Hebrews, see K. Schenck, "God Has Spoken," 321–36; and Treier, "Speech Acts," 337–50.

5. Buchanan, *Hebrews*, 61; Lane, *Hebrews 1–8*, 86.

6. Johnson, *Hebrews*, 113.

7. Ellingworth, *Hebrews*, 217; Koester, *Hebrews*, 263; Lane, *Hebrews 1–8*, 86; Witherington, *Letters and Homilies*, 171.

8. See ch. 4 above.

9. The reference in 10:15 is instructive in the author's understanding of the origin and authority of Scripture. Here, the text from Jeremiah is attributed to the Spirit speaking.

10:15 is on the redemption procured in the Son; the Spirit's place in the argumentation is to substantiate the assertions of the author.

In Heb 6:4–6, following a discussion in which the author chides his audience for not having advanced beyond the level of spiritual infancy (5:11–14) and exhorting them to move on toward perfection, leaving behind the foundational features of the faith (6:1–3), attention is turned toward a warning to avoid apostasy. The audience is addressed in a series of attributions in which the Spirit is placed in the center. They are described as having been enlightened, tasting the heavenly gift, sharing in the Holy Spirit, tasting the goodness of the word of God, and tasting of the powers of the age to come (vv. 4–5). Whether or not the reference to "enlightened" points to baptism and "tasted the heavenly gift" refers to the Eucharist,[10] the placement of the reference is suggestive. Whatever is meant by the first two attributions, they may be seen as informing what the author means by "shared in the Holy Spirit," with the final two attributions more fully developing this sharing.[11] Taken together, with the Spirit placed in the structural center of this complex, these attributions are largely evocative of the total redemption believers have experienced in the Son, with the Spirit demarcating those who belong to the community of the redeemed.[12] Hebrews 2:4, as we saw above, may be saying the same thing, namely, that the Spirit is distributed among those who have experienced the salvation of the Son. We will not enter into the tangled theological debates as to whether the author genuinely envisions the possibility that those who are so described may lose their salvation.[13] Rather, we are content to note that the Spirit in this passage is mentioned in the

---

However, in 8:8, it is God who is said to speak in the words of Jeremiah (a longer citation, 31:31–34).

10. Bruce, *Hebrews*, 145–46, supports this understanding, drawing on early attestation in the NT and early church (see footnotes 39–44 for references). Buchanan, *Hebrews*, 106, concurs, at least with reference to baptism, noting that reception of the Spirit was held to have occurred at baptism, or perhaps later with the laying on of hands. Other commentators, however, do not see this argument as compelling, e.g., Craddock, *Hebrews*, 75; and Lane, *Hebrews 1–8*, 143.

11. So Bruce, *Hebrews*, 145–47.

12. Attridge, *Hebrews*, 170; Buchanan, *Hebrews*, 106; Craddock, *Hebrews*, 75; Ellingworth, *Hebrews*, 315–20; Lane, *Hebrews 1–8*, 143; Witherington, *Letters*, 211–13.

13. The literature on this topic is voluminous. However, a convenient entry point into the issue may be found in Emmrich, "Hebrews 6:4–6," 83–95. His solution is derived from a study of second-temple Jewish literature in which the continued presence of the Spirit is connected with perseverance and obedience.

context of the salvation in the Son onto which the author is exhorting the audience to hold.

The reference to the Holy Spirit in Heb 9:8 is at first glance cut from the same cloth as those in 3:7 and 10:15. In this regard, Bruce suggests that the focus here is on the Spirit deriving significance from the words of Leviticus in which the rituals of the earthly tent are described.[14] That does not seem to be the most natural sense of the author's argumentation. Rather, in 9:8, the Spirit appears to provide a more contemporary lesson regarding the relationship between the old, earthly and the new, heavenly tents.[15] The Spirit is said to reveal that the earthly tent in which sacrifices are made is a symbol (*parabolē*) of the reality of the present situation in which the readers find themselves. The Spirit allows the understanding that the earthly tent actually obscures the heavenly tent into which Christ has offered himself as a sacrifice and has subsequently enabled access for believers, effectively preventing worshipers from experiencing the necessary cleansing of the conscience in its cultic practice.[16] The Spirit's revelation in this context again points to the redemptive work of Christ.

A few verses later, in 9:14, is a reference to the "eternal spirit" through which Christ offered himself as an unblemished sacrifice. There are three general ways in which the phrase "eternal Spirit" has been understood.[17] First, it is frequently understood to be a reference to the Holy Spirit. This was the predominant understanding of Roman Catholic teaching up until the twentieth century.[18] Second, predominant among Protestants intent on drawing attention to the merits of Christ's work alone in redemption and among many Roman Catholic thinkers during the twentieth century, is the view that it is a reference to the divinity of Christ.[19] Third, it may be understood as a reference to the mode or realm of the Spirit, the realm of God's existence, describing the realm into which Christ entered to of-

---

14. Bruce, *Hebrews*, 208. Koester, *Hebrews*, 405, seems to lean this direction, as does Ellingworth, *Hebrews*, 437.

15. Attridge, *Hebrews*, 240; Craddock, *Hebrews*, 104–5; O'Brien, *Hebrews*, 312.

16. Johnson, *Hebrews*, 224–25.

17. For discussion of the first two positions, see McGrath, "Through the Eternal Spirit," 1–2, 13–16, respectively.

18. So also several recent commentators, e.g., Bruce, *Hebrews*, 217; Craddock, *Hebrews*, 108; Ellingworth, *Hebrews*, 458; Lane, *Hebrews 9–13*, 241; O'Brien, *Hebrews*, 324–25; Witherington, *Letters*, 270–71.

19. So also Attridge, *Hebrews*, 251.

fer himself as a sacrifice.[20] At this stage, resolution of the problem is not important—we will argue below that seeing the "eternal spirit" as a reference to the Holy Spirit is the best understanding of the phrase. For now, it is sufficient to note the obvious context in which the reference is made, namely, as that through which Christ enters the heavenly sanctuary to offer himself as a sacrifice to offer the forgiveness of sins and the cleansing of the conscience. Again, the focus is on Christ's redemptive work.

The final reference to the Holy Spirit is in Heb 10:29. There is found another warning against apostasy in which those who fall away are described as "those who have spurned the Son of God, profaned the blood of the covenant by which they were sanctified, and outraged the Spirit of grace." Commentators frequently connect this passage with 9:14, in which it is through the Spirit that Christ has procured salvation, framed in terms of the grace given to believers that enables them to receive the cleansing of their consciences and access to the heavenly sanctuary.[21] In 10:29, mention of the Spirit as one of grace is associated with the Son and his blood offered in sacrifice, a clear connection between the Spirit and the redemptive work of the Son.

The path to observing anthropocentric bias in this presentation of the Spirit in Hebrews is illustrated clearly when viewed in light of the pneumatological thought of Jürgen Moltmann. A full picture of his pneumatology goes well beyond the scope of the present discussion.[22] We will focus primarily on a particular construct developed most fully in two of his works, *God in Creation* and *The Spirit of Life*. Moltmann distinguishes between two relationalities in connection with the persons of the Trinity: the relationship between the Father and the Spirit and the relationship between the Son and the Spirit. Broadly speaking, the relationship between Father and Spirit is understood in terms of creation, where God is present in creation through the life-giving Spirit, while the relationship between Son and Spirit is depicted in terms of the redemptive work of Christ. The

---

20. Johnson, *Hebrews*, 236. Craddock, *Hebrews*, 108, sees here a dual reference to the Holy Spirit and to the realm of Christ's sacrifice.

21. Attridge, *Hebrews*, 295; Johnson, *Hebrews*, 265; Koester, *Hebrews*, 457; Lane, *Hebrews 9–13*, 295. Ellingworth, *Hebrews*, 541, sees this reflected in the syntactical construction in which the adjectival sense is brought forward, "the gracious Spirit."

22. Helpful discussions of Moltmann's pneumatology may be found in Beck, *Holy Spirit*; and Neal, *Theology as Hope*.

first of these will occupy us below; here we will focus on the relationship of the Son and the Spirit in Moltmann's thought.

Moltmann further divides the relationship of Son and Spirit. He sees in the Synoptic portrayal of the relationship a Spirit christology, which he labels "Christ of the Spirit," whereas in Johannine and Pauline thought he sees a christological doctrine of the Spirit, which he labels "Spirit of Christ."[23] In the Synoptics, Jesus through the Spirit experienced himself as the messianic child and experienced God as beloved Father. The Spirit who came upon Jesus in his baptism fits him for his messianic mission, and in the person of Jesus, the Spirit experiences self-restriction and self-humiliation in its feeling identification with Jesus' person and history of life and suffering. So the path taken by Jesus is the path taken by the Spirit, and in Jesus' weakness the Spirit is proven strong. In commenting on Heb 9:14, Moltmann identifies the "eternal Spirit" as the Holy Spirit, the power that makes Jesus ready to surrender his life and that sustains this surrender. The Spirit is the indestructible life in whose power Jesus makes sacrifice on behalf of humanity. In short, the Synoptic depiction of Jesus' ministry is one in which the Spirit empowers Jesus to accomplish his redemptive ministry, up to and including death on the cross.[24]

With the resurrection of Jesus the focus shifts. It is through the Spirit that Christ is raised (cf. Rom 1:4), transferring this world into new creation. Following the resurrection of Christ, the relationship between Christ and the Spirit is labeled the "Spirit of Christ." The focus is on the risen Lord as the Spirit-sender who himself is present in the Spirit. The risen Christ is described as a "life-giving Spirit" (cf. 1 Cor 15:45), the one who lives from and in the eternal Spirit and the one in and through whom the Spirit of life acts for the redemption of the world. This Spirit poured out on all flesh is the *shekinah*[25] presence of God in the church, the body of Christ that sees itself as the down payment of new creation and the temple of the Holy Spirit, the community through and in which God's redemption of the cosmos is effected.[26]

23. Moltmann, *Spirit of Life*, 58–59.

24. Ibid., 61–64.

25. Ibid., 47, understands the *shekinah* as "the descent and indwelling of God in space and time, at a particular place and a particular era of earthly beings and in their history." This construct allows Moltmann to speak of God's presence in the Spirit in all of creation (*God in Creation*, 97), in the suffering of Jesus (*Spirit of Life*, 62), and in the church (*Spirit of Life*, 69).

26. Moltmann, *Spirit of Life*, 66–69.

In general, Moltmann describes here that aspect of pneumatology that is directly connected with the redemptive work of Christ on behalf of humanity. Of course, this is not the sum of his pneumatology. It is a construct derived from a piece of the biblical picture of the work of the Holy Spirit, a piece that we found evident in our overview of the references to the Holy Spirit in Hebrews. In that survey, we noticed first that there was a relative paucity of references to the Spirit in Hebrews, and that in those few references that are present, the Spirit is cast in a role that is rhetorically subordinate to the role of the Son in the argumentation. In the biblical depiction, then, we see a dual level of anthropocentric bias. First, the relative lack of references to the Spirit demonstrates a bias in favor of christology over pneumatology, and the christology of Hebrews, as we have argued elsewhere,[27] is one that is focused largely on the benefits of the Son's saving work on behalf of human beings. And second, the few references we see to the Holy Spirit are offered in material support of these same christological and soteriological emphases of the rhetoric. At both levels, anthropocentric biases are present in both the mode and substance of the references to the Spirit.

This tendency in Hebrews is paralleled in subsequent, particularly Western, traditions of theological reflection. Moltmann argues that in the doctrine of the *filioque*, a subordinationistic tendency emerges in which the Spirit is viewed as the "Spirit of Christ," a Spirit of redemption.[28] This viewpoint obscures the connection of the Spirit with creation emphasized in Moltmann's description of the relationship of Father and Spirit. Here the focus settles squarely on the human benefits of the redemptive work of Christ. No case is being made here for a genetic relationship between the pattern found in Hebrews and the subsequent pattern found in the doctrine of the *filioque*. Rather, what is seen in both is a bias that restricts the scope of pneumatology to the redemptive benefit for human beings. It is the composition of a vocal piece in which the Spirit is relegated to a minor harmonic voice in support of the dominant voices in the choir.

Given this bias, it remains to establish a point of identification between human beings and the other than human creation in the depiction of the Holy Spirit in Hebrews. To that we now turn our attention.

---

27. See ch. 2 above.
28. Moltmann, *Spirit of Life*, 9.

IDENTIFICATION: THROUGH THE "ETERNAL SPIRIT"

As noted above, the phrase "eternal spirit" in Heb 9:14 is open to diverse interpretation. It may refer to the Holy Spirit, to the divinity of Christ, or to the realm or mode in which Christ offered himself a sacrifice. In order to establish an identification between human beings and Earth in light of the pneumatology of Hebrews, we will first establish that the reference to "eternal spirit" in 9:14 is best understood as a reference to the Holy Spirit.

The first line of evidence is observed in the manuscript tradition. Some witnesses (א² D* Π *al* it vg bo) have the reading "holy" instead of "eternal." While the weight of the evidence certainly sides with reading "eternal" as original,[29] the variant demonstrates that relatively early in the thinking of the church the notion that the Holy Spirit is the referent in the passage seemed natural.

Some have argued that a theological reading of the passage shows a trinitarian structure to the passage.[30] In this line of thought, the progression of the offering described in the passage argues for such a reading: Christ (the Son) offers himself as a sacrifice through the eternal (read "Holy") Spirit unblemished to God (the Father). This position has its critics on the grounds that a robust trinitarian viewpoint is unsustainable in light of the diffuse and undeveloped pneumatology in Hebrews.[31] Nevertheless, such thinking is evidence of how easily subsequent interpreters came to make the connection to the Holy Spirit in the passage.

A more sustainable line of argumentation is to understand why the designation "eternal" is appropriate in the context if indeed the referent is the Holy Spirit.[32] Throughout the letter-sermon, the author has been at pains to demonstrate that the sacrifices of the old covenant were ineffectual because they produced only a temporary, ceremonial sanctification (9:6–7, 13, 25; 10:1–4, 10, 12). A significant part of the author's rhetoric attests to the superiority of the Son's sacrifice because the effects of this sacrifice are eternal, precisely due to the faultless, unblemished sacrifice

---

29. Lane, *Hebrews 9–13*, 230, argues that "Holy Spirit" is clearly a secondary reading derived from early conviction that "eternal spirit" was a periphrasis for "Holy Spirit."

30. See discussion in McGrath, *"Through the Eternal Spirit,"* 94–96.

31. Attridge, *Hebrews*, 251.

32. The following discussion summarizes McGrath, *"Through the Eternal Spirit,"* 90–103.

of the Son (9:14, 28; 10:10). The reason such a sacrifice is necessary is so that the consciences of the worshipers might be made pure so that they might serve the living God (9:9, 14; 10:14) and have access to the heavenly sanctuary (10:19–22; cf. 4:16). Such a sacrifice must be offered by a priest who is of an eternal order (5:6; 6:20; 7:15–22). However, the author of Hebrews also argues for the humanity of Jesus, the high priest of this eternal order, so that he might offer such a sacrifice in sympathy with human beings (2:14–18; 4:15; 5:7–8). Given the sinfulness of human priests and the concomitant ineffectiveness of their sacrifices, how might the human Jesus be fit to be both an eternal high priest as well as the unblemished sacrifice? The answer is that in his messianic ministry he is the one endowed with the power of the Spirit for the performance of his mission in the sense of the Isaianic servant of the Lord (cf. Isa 42:1; 61:1).[33] It is by the presence and power of the Holy Spirit that the man Jesus is sanctified for both his priestly service and his sacrificial offering. In his earthly ministry, the Son submitted his life and humanity to the sanctifying power of the Holy Spirit.

If it is by the power of the Spirit that the Son performs his priestly ministry, why the qualifier "eternal"? Simply put, the designation of the Holy Spirit as eternal fits with the strategy of argumentation throughout Hebrews, where "eternal" is repeatedly played off against the earthly, temporal nature of the old covenant. If the priesthood and redemption secured by the Son are classified as eternal, and this priesthood and redemption are established through the sanctification of the Holy Spirit, then the designation of the Holy Spirit as the eternal Spirit is quite natural,[34] in keeping with the tendency exhibited by the author throughout Hebrews.[35]

So it is at least plausible that the "eternal spirit" of Heb 9:14 refers to the Holy Spirit. Arguing that point is one thing; the remaining question is how this helps forge an identification between human beings and Earth. To this we now turn our attention.

33. So Bruce, *Hebrews*, 217; Lane, *Hebrews 9–13*, 241. Lane argues that the passage in Hebrews is laden with allusions to Isaiah, so the connection of the "eternal spirit" with the Holy Spirit is appropriate here.

34. So Koester, *Hebrews*, 410; cf. Heb 9:12.

35. McGrath, "Through the Eternal Spirit," 96–102, employs an intertextual argument at this point. He notes that Heb 7:16 asserts that a change in priesthood brings about a change in law. Based on Rom 8:2, the new law in effect is the law of the Holy Spirit. So by conforming his human will to this new law on which his priestly being is established, Christ may freely offer the perfect sacrifice of his own life (103).

The discussion in Hebrews leading to the statement in question in v. 14 has since v. 1 been concerned with a comparison of tents, or sanctuaries, in which the sacrifices in view are offered. Integral to this discussion are the comparisons between the coordinate priesthoods and the offerings of blood in the sanctuaries. It is tempting to ask precisely at which point in Christ's career is the offering of his blood made: at the cross, where he actually died and his blood was spilled, or in heaven, presumably following the ascension, where he brought his blood into the heavenly sanctuary.[36] But for our purposes, a more pertinent question arises. What is it that was offered in this sacrifice? As stated explicitly in the passage, it is the blood of the man Jesus, and implicitly, his body as well.

As mentioned earlier, the author of Hebrews has argued pointedly that Jesus was indeed a genuine human being, a proposition that is fundamental to the logic of the argumentation. As the argumentation proceeds forward from 9:14 into ch. 10, within a discussion of the inefficacy of the sacrifices of "blood of bulls and goats" to take away sins, the author cites and alters Ps 39:6–8 (LXX) to the effect that in place of such sacrifices under the old covenant, God has given a body to Christ as he entered the world so that he might do God's will (Heb 10:4–5). The point for our purposes is that it is in his embodiment that the Son will perform God's will in providing the unblemished sacrifice of his blood. So the perfect sacrifice by the perfect priest in the perfect sanctuary involves the materiality and physicality of the body and blood of the Son.

Moreover, this offering of the body and blood of Christ is offered in connection with the Spirit, as made evident in Heb 9:14. In offering his body and blood through the eternal Spirit, a connection between human beings and Earth is forged. In this offering the same Spirit depicted in Hebrews as working in concert with the Son to secure redemption for human beings is shown to be the Spirit connected to materiality as well. As we noted in an earlier chapter (ch. 2), the same human physicality birthed from Earth (cf. Gen 2:7) is the stuff that the Son shared in his incarnation (Heb 2:14), forging a strong identification between human beings and Earth. With Heb 9:14, the Holy Spirit is drawn into the complex as a further point of identification between human beings and Earth.

---

36. Davidson, "Sinlessness of Jesus Christ," 390–91, makes the case that the Spirit is the one who not only sanctifies Christ to be the unblemished sacrifice but who also empowers Christ to walk the path of suffering and obedience unto the cross. Cf. Moltmann, *Spirit of Life*, 61–62, for a similar understanding.

Moltmann's understanding of the relationship between Son and Spirit is helpful in elucidating the Spirit's place in the identification of human beings and Earth. In his category of "Christ of the Spirit," the Spirit empowers Jesus of Nazareth for his ministry, which is concerned with both human beings and nature. Healings of physical bodies and miracles that brought order to chaotic natural phenomena (e.g., calming the storm) are instances where by virtue of the power of the Holy Spirit the man Jesus demonstrates concern for both human beings and other than human creation. The category "Spirit of Christ" entails the ascended man Jesus, the Spirit-baptizer, pouring out the Holy Spirit upon the earth. We will speak more of this in a later chapter (ch. 6), but for now suffice it to say that the ascended Jesus reigns over the world in the Spirit in anticipation of the time that heaven and earth will come together in new creation. What this shows is that the relationship between Son and Spirit is not simply reducible to redemptive benefits for human beings only. Further reflection in light of the categories described by Moltmann shows that given the tendency to view the Spirit in subordinate support of the redemptive work of the Son on behalf of human beings, a broader view of the relationship of Son and Spirit is possible, one that involves forging a connection between human beings and other than human creation. This is also the case with the relationship of Son and Spirit in Heb 9:14.

Perhaps the apostle Paul best characterizes the connection we are trying to establish between human beings and Earth in a series of statements in Romans. The Spirit through which Christ is raised bodily from the dead (1:4) and through which our mortal bodies will be raised (8:11) is also the Spirit who groans along with human beings and the whole of creation in anticipation of redemption (8:18–27). The redemptive work accomplished by Christ for the benefit of human beings is also directed toward the whole of creation, a fact attested by the sympathetic anticipatory groaning of the Spirit with all components of creation. The Spirit's agency in the work of redemption entails ramifications for human and other than human creation alike. So the Spirit is a significant aspect of that which binds human beings to Earth in empathetic connection. In language appropriate to the context, that is a connection we might tease out of Heb 9:14.

Having established a point of identification between human beings and Earth in light of the depiction of the Spirit in Heb 9:14, what might the voice of Earth speak with regard to the role of the Spirit, particularly

A Whispered Voice in the Choir 63

in connection with Earth? We address this question in the final section of this discussion.

RETRIEVAL: ASSERTING THE WHISPERED VOICE IN THE CHOIR

We noted earlier that Moltmann describes the role of the Spirit in terms of a pair of relationships: Spirit and Son, and Spirit and Father. In this construction, the Spirit in connection with the Son, particularly in what Moltmann called the "Spirit of Christ," is a conception focused primarily on the Spirit's role in effecting redemption for human beings. Set alongside this conception of the Spirit in Moltmann's thinking is the "Spirit of God," or the "Spirit of the Father," which is cast primarily in terms of creation. The "Spirit of Christ" emphasis in Western theology, particularly seen through the prism of the *filioque* doctrine, has tended to view creation primarily in terms of the stage upon which is played out the drama of human redemption, a view held incorrect by Moltmann in light of the coordinate biblical emphasis on the "Spirit of God."[37] So integral to uncovering the voice of Earth in the scant pneumatology of Hebrews is a recovery of the biblical emphasis on the "Spirit of God."

For Moltmann, creation is a trinitarian process, not simply a singular act of the Father. Creation unfolds in three stages. First is the original act of creation *ex nihilo*, which is oriented toward the eschatological future when God will take up creation as God's dwelling place. Second is the ongoing creation in which God's presence in the Spirit sustains creation and moves it toward eschatological redemption. And third is the new creation of all things.[38] In this process, God the Father creates through the Son in the Spirit; Christ mediates creation, while the Holy Spirit represents God's *shekinah* presence in creation through which God enters into the struggles, victories, and sufferings of the entire creation all the while keeping all things in life by God's pneumatological presence in creation.[39] This Trinitarian emphasis in the initial, ongoing, and new creation of all things leads to a perception of God in all things and all things in God based on the theological understanding of the "Spirit of God" as the power of

---

37. Moltmann, *God in Creation*, 5, 55, 166, 277.
38. For summary, see Beck, *Holy Spirit*, 111–12.
39. Moltmann, *God in Creation*, xiv, 97.

creation and wellspring of life (cf. Job 33:4; 34:13–14; Ps 104:29–30).[40] Moltmann labels this construction "immanent transcendence," where God is distinct from creation but is nevertheless present within it. It is in the Spirit that the transcendent God is made immanent in creation, forging a type of perichoretic love between God and creation.[41] It is this pneumatological presence of God in creation, according to Moltmann, that is the basis for a Christian doctrine of ecology.[42]

For Moltmann, a crucial point is the understanding that the "Spirit of Christ" for redemption is the self-same "Spirit of God" in creation. The bridge that connects these two conceptions is the redemption itself. Under the influence of the *filioque* doctrine the role of the Holy Spirit has effectively been reduced to the role of the "Spirit of Christ" in the redemption of the human soul. However, the Trinitarian framing of the creative process—initial, ongoing, and new—demonstrates that the Spirit is active in both the present experience of creation as well as in the unfolding of new creation. In the initial act of creation God had in view the eschatological future of creation becoming the dwelling place of God. Indeed, this notion of creation being redeemed from its present decay and corruption and fitted for God's dwelling is found in the New Testament (e.g., Col 1:20; Rom 8:19–21; Rev 21–22). If Christ is seen as the one through whom creation has come into being (e.g., Col 1:16; Heb 1:2), and he is the one through whom redemption for the cosmos is secured (e.g., Col 1:20), and he is the one who sustains the cosmos by his presence (e.g., Col 1:16; Heb 1:3), then wherever Christ is present so too is the Spirit. And if Christ's redemption is seen in terms of the resurrection of the body and the renewal of all things, and this is understood as the activity of the life-giving Spirit, then in reality, the "Spirit of Christ" is none other than the "Spirit of God."[43]

So how does this discourse on Moltmann's conception of the "Spirit of God" help us retrieve the voice of Earth? In light of this discussion, Earth might assert that one implication of the depiction of the Spirit in Hebrews is that its few discussions of the Spirit in support of the christology and soteriology of Hebrews bring to mind the flipside of the biblical

---

40. Moltmann, *Spirit of Life*, 35.
41. Moltmann, *God in Creation*, 15–17.
42. Ibid., 12.
43. Moltmann, *Spirit of Life*, 8–9.

portrayal of the Spirit, namely, the place of the Spirit with respect to creation. Stated another way, Earth might assert that there is no escape, even in light of the biases of the author of Hebrews in the depiction of the Spirit strictly in terms of the rhetorical interests of the argumentation, from the implication that in the Spirit the creation, sustenance, and redemption of Earth is a necessary corollary to the redemption of human beings. As we saw in our discussion of the identification between human beings and Earth, even in a passage such as Heb 9:14, where the focus was squarely on the redemptive efficacy of the sacrifice of Christ for human beings, materiality was essential to that which was offered through the "eternal Spirit."

The voice of Earth might also sharpen the focus of its call to consider the "Spirit of God" in creation as one considers the "Spirit of Christ" in redemption by articulating precisely what this focus on the "Spirit of God" entails for Earth. In truth what we see here is that as the conception of the "Spirit of God" melds together with the conception of the "Spirit of Christ," our conception of the very redemption wrought through Christ must expand to include Earth as well as human beings. But how does the Spirit fit in with the redemption of Earth? We noted earlier that in Romans Paul draws on the imagery of groaning to speak of the response of the Spirit in concert with the groaning of both human beings and the other than human creation as they await their joint redemption from corruption and decay (cf. Rom 8:19–27).[44] With this starting point in view, Pentecostal theologian Macchia frames an understanding of the Spirit's present work in creation that draws attention to the eschatological goal of preparing creation to be the final dwelling place of God.[45] Focal to Macchia's project is the understanding that Jesus was in his earthly ministry the Spirit-empowered Messiah who proclaimed God's will through the Spirit (Matt 12:28), and that this same Jesus was raised into new life by the power of the Spirit (Rom 1:4) in order to impart the Spirit, not only to those who would believe but also into all creation.[46] Macchia makes much of the words of Gregory of Nyssa: "The Spirit is a living and a substantial and distinctly subsisting kingdom with which the only begotten Christ

44. Solivan, *Spirit*, argues from a Hispanic Pentecostal perspective that Pentecostal spirituality is a pathos in which human beings groan in solidarity with a suffering creation in the Spirit.

45. Macchia, *Baptized in the Spirit*, 102–3.

46. Ibid., 109–10.

is anointed and is king of all that is."⁴⁷ Gregory's words, according to Macchia, imply that Christ is the King and the Spirit itself is the Kingdom to the end that Christ reigns over all creation in the Spirit who fills all creation. Spirit baptism, that is, the imparting of the Spirit into the world by the risen Son, then, is that through which the reign of the creating Father, the crucified and risen Son, and life-giving presence of the Spirit work to "liberate creation from within history toward new possibilities for free, eschatological existence."⁴⁸

Other scholars offer similar characterizations of the Spirit's present work in creation. Boff speaks of the current ministry of the Holy Spirit as the "pneumatizing" of creation toward its redemption from death and as uniting creation once again with the life of the Trinity.⁴⁹ Pinnock focuses on the "cosmic operation of the Spirit" that sees the divine acts of creation and redemption as integral to the Spirit's work, such that the "Spirit is the ecstasy of divine life, the overabundance of joy, that gives birth to the universe and ever works to bring about a fullness of unity."⁵⁰ The Spirit, by virtue of its presence in all phases of creation—initial, ongoing, and new—is central to the redemptive work of Christ that entails all of creation. This pneumatological thread running through the history of the cosmos constitutes a refining of the call of Earth to consider the conception of the "Spirit of God" as the vital counterpart of the "Spirit of Christ" emphasis in the thinly developed pneumatology of Hebrews.

The voice of Earth might offer one further refinement of the "Spirit of God" emphasis. Earth might remind us of Moltmann's assertion, noted earlier, that it is the pneumatological presence of God in creation that forms the basis of a Christian doctrine of ecology. In a recent article, another Pentecostal scholar, Clifton, argues that a proper appreciation of the full work of the Spirit in creation and redemption should lead Christians to understand that the presence of the Spirit in all creation is a Spirit of life that encompasses both the present creation and the eschatological new creation. In fact, the present work of the Spirit is the movement of creation toward new creation in a transformative process that finally eventuates in the eschatological kingdom of God. Spirit-filled believers

47. Gregory of Nyssa, *On the Lord's Prayer* 3, cited and discussed in Macchia, *Baptized in the Spirit*, 89.

48. Macchia, *Baptized in the Spirit*, 89, 97.

49. Boff, *Cry of the Earth*, 271.

50. Pinnock, *Flame of Love*, 48–51.

should see a Spirit-filled Earth (cf. Ps 139:7–9) as a way of overcoming the fundamental separation of human beings from the other than human creation that has characterized much post-Enlightenment Western thought, including Christian theology, thus leading to a Spirit-empowered participation in the redemption of Earth in anticipation of its eschatological destiny.[51] Earth calls the Spirit-filled community of believers in the church to recognize that the Spirit fills all creation with the presence of divine life and to participate in the liberation of Earth from its present corruption through ecological action.

To summarize, retrieval of the voice of Earth entails recognition that the scant pneumatology of Hebrews, restricted as it is on a presentation of what Moltmann calls the "Spirit of Christ" for the redemption of human beings, by necessity implies Moltmann's construct of the "Spirit of God" in creation. This creational aspect of the Spirit's work suggests that the presence of the Spirit saturates all of creation in all phases of creation—initial, ongoing, new—directing creation in its totality toward eschatological transformation into the dwelling place of God. This Spirit saturation of creation further suggests that Spirit-filled believers should identify with Earth in its groanings and sufferings and also seek to alleviate Earth's experience of suffering in anticipation of eschatological glory through ecologically conscientious action. If in Hebrews the Spirit is the whispered voice in the choir, and its voice harmonizes with the dominant strains of the christological and soteriological interests of the composer, then what Earth suggests here is perhaps best seen as another layer of harmony that provides richer textures to the dominant voices in the choir.

CONCLUSION

Obviously pneumatology is not a major concern in its own right in Hebrews. Direct references are few, and those that are present have a decidedly narrow focus in support of other themes in the argumentation. The tack taken in this discussion was simply to tease out the broader implications of pneumatology given the contours of Spirit talk in Hebrews. The entry point into such a discussion was a closer examination of one verse, 9:14, in which an opening was found within what is admittedly a christological and soteriological discussion. Here the role of the Spirit

---

51. See Clifton, "Preaching the 'Full Gospel,'" 117–34; and Tallman, "Pentecostal Ecology," 135–54.

betrayed a deep connection with the materiality of the created world even within a context where that is clearly not the author's intended exploration. From this point we were able to explore further pneumatological ramifications of the connection between the Spirit and Earth. At the end of the day, we are not much closer to a more developed pneumatology of Hebrews. But perhaps we are closer to demonstrating that Hebrews, with its unique argumentation and mode of presentation, is not as inimical to an Earth-friendly reading as the surface features of its rhetoric first suggests.

6

"He Has Prepared a City for Them" (Hebrews 11:16)

Escapist Eschatology or Ecological Expedience?

INTRODUCTION

IN HEB 11:8–16, THE author commends Abraham for his faith, citing the example of Abraham's setting out from his home country to an unknown land in obedience to the command of God. The author notes that Abraham settled for a time in the land that had been given him in the promise, but that he did so as a stranger and alien upon the earth (v. 9). The focus of the author is not on Abraham or his posterity receiving the promised land, but is rather on an eschatological interpretation of the promised homeland that is aimed at exhorting the readers of the letter-sermon to keep their eyes fixed on the eternal reward of perseverance. Thus the example of Abraham is but one of many in ch. 11 that urges the readers to look beyond their present circumstances to the eschatological promise of eternal life.

Frequently, however, this passage among others in Hebrews (e.g., 1:10–12; 4:1–11; 12:22–28) is used to justify an escapist eschatology that minimizes attention on the present order and its afflictions in favor of a rather singular focus on the world to come. If indeed believers are strangers and foreigners upon the earth, living as those just passing through, with eyes fixed on the eternal city God has prepared for them, then believers may be justified to pay little attention to a homeland not their own. Cadwallader's stark appraisal captures the stakes of the present discussion: "Previous interpretations that have rendered Earth obsolete become exposed as reading choices transmitting disastrous ecological consequences and ethical immunities on their perpetrators."[1]

This study will attempt to put the passage into proper perspective by viewing its teaching in terms of the larger context of the argumentative strategy of the author of Hebrews. The conclusion will affirm the integrity of Heb 11:8–16 within its own rhetorical context while examining how the rhetoric need not lead to an escapist eschatology that disregards care for the created order in the present. The principles of ecological hermeneutics developed by the Consultation on Ecological Hermeneutics Section in the Society of Biblical Literature—suspicion, identification, retrieval—will form the shape of this study.

ESCAPIST ESCHATOLOGY—SUSPICION OF A BIAS AGAINST THE EARTH

Before we investigate how Hebrews might depict an escapist eschatology, it behooves us to define what we mean by escapist eschatology. An escapist eschatology is one in which the putative goal of history for the faithful is to be removed from the present order replete with its fallenness to a state of bliss. Typically, but not necessarily, this escapism is cast in terms of the destruction of the present created order, with the faithful spending eternity in the presence of God in heaven. Historians and exegetes often ascribe the source of this type of eschatology to the influence of Hellenistic and sometimes Gnostic cosmologies on the biblical pictures of the future.[2] The net effect of such an escapist mentality on ecology is not hard to surmise. It results in indifference toward care for the created order on the one hand, and justification for exploitation of creation for economic gains on the other.

The letter-sermon of Hebrews is frequently seen as advancing an escapist eschatology. The history of interpretation of Hebrews has been mired in analyses aimed at determining the intellectual background of its argument. Various sources—Platonism, Philonism, Jewish apocalyptic, Gnosticism, to name a few—are put forth as the basis of the dualism central in Hebrews that gives rise to the contention that the present created order is destined for destruction in favor of a heavenly reality to come.

---

1. Cadwallader, "Earth as Host," 149.
2. This is the contention, e.g., of Wright, *Surprised by Hope*, who subjects this sort of escapism to scathing critique.

While the source of the background to the argument of Hebrews is in all likelihood beyond recovery due to the paucity of data regarding its composition—authorship, date, audience, exigence[3]—there is no doubt that dualistic categories are prominent in the argument and lend strength to the assertion that the letter-sermon advances an escapist eschatology.

Two trajectories run throughout Hebrews that contribute to its eschatology. One such trajectory might be labeled a trajectory of "rest."[4] Three passages in Hebrews form the structure of this trajectory: 4:1–11; 10:19–25; and 12:22–24. In each case, a significant aspect of the old covenant is relativized through a comparison with the superiority of the Son as bringer of the new covenant, resulting in a reinterpretation of the literal feature of the old covenant in terms of the work of the Son. In 4:1–11, the promise of the land given to Abraham and realized by Joshua is reshaped into the Sabbath rest enjoyed by God following the work of creation and made available to believers in the Son. The actual land itself is no longer the focus of the promise; the promise is fulfilled in the person of the Son.[5] The next passage, 10:19–25, describes the believer's rest as access to God via entry into the holiest part of the heavenly sanctuary, an access enabled by the priesthood and sacrifice of the Son. Here the substance of the Israelite cultus is rendered obsolete by way of the entrance of the perfect priest with the perfect sacrifice into the perfect sanctuary. The final passage of the trajectory, 12:22–24, characterizes the rest of believers as eternal life, the culmination of which is entry into the heavenly Jerusalem. While the obvious contrast is with the earthly Jerusalem, the context of the passage indicates that the contrast in view is with Mt. Sinai and the fearfulness surrounding reception of the old covenant. The eternal destination of believers, in contrast, is variously identified as Mount Zion, the city of the living God, the heavenly Jerusalem, populated with innumerable angels in festal gathering, the assembly of the firstborn who are enrolled in heaven, God the judge of all, the spirits of the righteous made perfect, Jesus the mediator of a new covenant, and the sprinkled blood that speaks a better word than the blood of Abel.

---

3. Schenck, *Cosmology and Eschatology*, ch. 2, argues that it is methodologically flawed to begin with a discussion of the background of Hebrews and then explain the argument in light of this reconstruction. His approach is to examine the content of the argument to deduce what can be said about the background.

4. Koester, *Hebrews*, 276.

5. See ch. 4 above.

The net effect of the trajectory of rest is a type of spiritualization of earthly realities into corresponding heavenly realities. The location of our passage, 11:8–16, between the final two passages of the trajectory, casts the story of Abraham's pilgrimage firmly within a heavenly orientation, anticipatory of the heavenly destination described in 12:22–24. Abraham's quest for a homeland is a quest for a heavenly destination. The relativization of the land begun in 4:1–11 is advanced in 11:8–16, with the exclamation point of the argument occurring in 12:22–24. The rest awaiting believers is a heavenly rest, one not found on earth.

The second trajectory, which will occupy most of our attention, might be labeled a trajectory of "transience of the created order."[6] Again, three passages are prominent: 1:10–12; our passage, 11:8–16; 12:18–29.[7] The first text, 1:10–12, is a citation of Ps 102 [101 LXX]:26–28. Here the text is applied to the Son (cf. 1:8a) as a demonstration of the Son's eternality in the extended contrast of the Son with the angels (vv. 4–14). However, the language of the psalm itself describes God and God's attributes as eternal in comparison with the transitory universe that God has created.[8] Though not the primary point of the passage, the transitory nature of the created universe is introduced into the argumentation of Hebrews.

Hebrews 11:8–16 draws out with explicit clarity the transitory character of the created cosmos. Several details in the passage suggest this. First is the characterization of Abraham as acting on faith. Abraham is said to have left his homeland "by faith" (*pistei*, v. 8) and to have dwelt as a stranger in the land of promise "by faith" (v. 9). He, along with Isaac and Jacob, is said to have died "in faith" (*kata pistin*, v. 13) not having received the promise, but rather having seen it and welcomed it from afar, confessing that they were "strangers" and "refugees" on the earth. This depiction of Abraham as a person characterized by faith is established by 11:1, in which faith is defined in terms of the future, as the "assurance of things hoped for" (*elpizomenōn hypostasis*) and the "conviction of things

---

6. Schenck, *Cosmology and Eschatology*, 122–32.

7. While the passages noted here are explicitly directed to the transience of the created order, Schenck, *Cosmology and Eschatology*, 131–32, suggests that Heb 9:8–9, in its discussion of the earthly tent as a "parable" of two ages, assigns the meaning of the outer tent to the earthly cosmos while the Holy of Holies in the earthly sanctuary represents the heavenly sanctuary that remains unseen while the outer tent still stands. This implies that there will come a time when the outer tent, and parabolically the earthly cosmos, passes away.

8. Attridge, *Hebrews*, 381.

not seen" (*pragmatōn elegchos ou blepomenōn*). The obedience Abraham demonstrated in responding to the call of God has been recast by the author of Hebrews to reflect confidence in the eschatological inheritance awaiting those who respond to God "by faith."[9]

Moreover, Abraham is characterized by terminology that casts him in the role of a "resident alien" with respect to his relationship to this world.[10] He is described as "living as a stranger" (*parōkēsen*, v. 9), as a "foreigner dwelling in tents" (*allotrian en skēnais katoikēsas*, v. 9), and along with Isaac and Jacob (and Sarah?) as "strangers" (*xenoi*, v. 13) and "refugees" (*parepidēmoi*, v. 13). As it stands, this language alone does not necessitate an otherworldly orientation. However, it is with respect to the land promised to Abraham that he so dwelled as a resident alien, for he is said to have died not receiving the promise for which he was looking (v. 13). So what is the promise for which he longed? He awaited "the city that has foundations, whose architect and builder is God" (v. 10). The author of Hebrews will explicitly identify this city as the heavenly Jerusalem in 12:22, though in several strands of roughly contemporary Jewish tradition this city is likewise identified as the heavenly Jerusalem that will be revealed in the end times (4 *Ezra* 7:26; 8:52; 10:27; cf. Rev 21:2, 10), while Philo (*Leg.* 3:83; *Somn.* 2:250) and some Jewish apocalyptic sources (e.g., 2 *En.* 55:2) characterize this city as a transcendent reality, and other tradition sees it as prepared from the foundation of the world and revealed to Adam, Abraham, and Moses (2 *Bar.* 4:1–4). This characterization of Abraham and the promise effectively removes the emphasis from the literal fulfillment of God's promise to Abraham as the land of Canaan to a future fulfillment that is defined in terms of a heavenly reality.

Another detail in the passage that contributes to a transitory understanding of the created order is somewhat subtle. In 11:8, the author of Hebrews has apparently made a conscious change in his appropriation of Gen 12:1 (LXX). The substitution of *topos* for *gē* serves to reframe the orientation of promise beyond considerations of historical geography to "an inheritance transcendent in character."[11] The placement of this substitution at the beginning of the passage sets the thematic parameters for understanding the remainder of the passage.

---

9. Craddock, *Hebrews*, 136, describes this reshaping of the Abraham tradition as a "Christian interpretation" of the story.

10. Koester, *Hebrews*, 485.

11. Lane, *Hebrews 9–13*, 349; cf. Craddock, *Hebrews*, 136.

One final detail for consideration has to do with the forward-looking direction of the patriarchs in 11:15. As they searched for a homeland, they did not look backwards, though the opportunity to do so would have been a very real possibility. In the ancient world, the search for a homeland often directed sojourners back to their land of origin.[12] However, the author here quite pointedly asserts that Abraham set his gaze straight ahead, rejecting the possibility for an earthly fulfillment of the promise.

At this point, we might justly ask whether Heb 11:8–16 truly constitutes an affirmation of the transitory nature of the created order, and thus contributes to the escapist eschatology that is alleged in the passage. On its own, perhaps it is not necessary to see such in the passage. One could conceivably see the seeds of an escapist eschatology in the characterization of Abraham et al. as those who seek their destiny in future, heavenly terms. But does this imply the transitoriness of the order they seek to move beyond? It is in viewing the passage as part of a trajectory that the transitory nature of the created order is implicit in Heb 11:8–16. What is implicit in this passage is made explicit in Heb 12:18–29.

Hebrews 12:18–29 occurs within the larger context of a warning to the readers not to follow the path of Esau, who forsook his place of blessing and was thus unable to secure restoration (vv. 15–17). The author highlights that the severity of the judgment that those under the old covenant experienced for disobedience pales in comparison with that to come upon those who reject the blessings of the new covenant of the Son. From here, the author enters into a comparison of two mountains, Sinai and Zion. The first mount, Sinai, is characterized in foreboding terms, with the fearful response of the people receiving emphasis. Three details are noteworthy in this description, the first two of which are closely related. First, the description of the sight at Mt. Sinai is descriptive of the terrible manifestation of the presence and holiness of God, particularly through the sound of the trumpet and the voice, amidst a people not holy enough to bear the sight (vv. 18–21). Second, and related, the fear of the people is representatively reflected in the words of Moses who claims to be "trembling" (*entromos*, v. 21) with fear. And third, this mountain is described as one that can be touched (*psēlaphōmenō*, v. 18).

The final of these details, describing Sinai as that which can be touched, sets up the contrast with Mt. Zion, which is identified as the

---

12. Koester, *Hebrews*, 497–98; Craddock, *Hebrews*, 137.

heavenly Jerusalem and is described in quite otherworldly terms (vv. 22–24). So the goal toward which Abraham was described as striving, and toward which the readers of Hebrews are striving as well, is a transcendent reality.

The first two details describing the Sinai scene are anticipatory of the shaking described in vv. 25–29.[13] Whereas God shook the earth at Sinai, once more God will shake not just the earth, but also the heavens (v. 26). The author cites and modifies Hag 2:6 to highlight the judgment associated with the Day of the Lord, bringing into focus the upcoming contrast between heaven and earth.[14] A pair of terms in this section describing the outcome of this shaking emphasize this contrast. Heaven will remain (*menō*) while the earth will be removed (*metathesis*). While commentators attempt to identify the background to this formulation,[15] the passage makes clear that the distinctive criterion in the outcome of the shaking is whether the things in view are created or heavenly in nature (12:27). That which remains is the heavenly kingdom to be inherited by believers (v. 28).

Let us bring this section of our discussion to a conclusion. We set out to identify a bias against Earth in Heb 11:8–16. To do so, we observed a couple of trajectories in Hebrews in which an otherworldly emphasis emerged in conjunction with a focus on the transitory nature of the created order. We observed the place of Heb 11:8–16 within both of these trajectories to ascertain how the passage functions in them. The path our study followed is best reflected in the conclusions reached by Schenck in his recent study of Hebrews. Schenck sees the author of Hebrews employing a cosmological and eschatological dualism to accomplish the author's rhetorical purpose of contrasting Christ with the Levitical order, assigning Christ's work to enduring heavenly categories while identifying the Levitical order with earthly categories that are passing away.[16] The result-

---

13. Koester, *Hebrews*, 552.

14. Lane, *Hebrews 9–13*, 480.

15. Ellingworth, *Hebrews*, 685–89, locates it in a cosmology that divides the universe into upper and lower parts, where the lower part is removed in this shaking. Attridge, *Hebrews*, 381, sees a strand of Jewish apocalyptic in view where the annihilation of the created universe takes place on the basis of an opposition between flesh and spirit. Johnson, *Hebrews*, 335, identifies a Platonic background, though modified from a strict matter/spirit duality to an opposition between created things and things that participate in God.

16. Schenck, *Cosmology and Eschatology*, 115–17.

ing argumentation produces, at least unconsciously, a view of the created order as something that is flawed and from which humanity needs to be saved, something that was always destined for destruction once its role in staging God's redemptive purposes has played out.[17] But in light of this reading, which it must be admitted has been of common currency in the history of the interpretation of Hebrews, we must seriously entertain the possibility of Buchanan's charge that this reading is more a reflection of the interpreter's theological biases than it is the position of the author of Hebrews.[18] In other words, granted that interpreters have frequently understood Hebrews generally, and 11:8–16 specifically, in this way, is another reading possible? To that prospect we now turn our attention.

EARTH: HERE AS IT IS IN HEAVEN—
IDENTIFICATION THROUGH RESURRECTION

Hebrews 11:8–16 is not our author's final word about Abraham in the present context. In vv. 17–19 the author draws another datum from the biblical tradition concerning Abraham to demonstrate his faithfulness to God: the sacrifice of Isaac. In v. 19, however, the author ascribes to Abraham a motivation that goes beyond the story in Gen 22. The author describes Abraham as one who considered that God is able to raise the dead, and on this basis, he can respond in faith to the command of God to sacrifice Isaac, the channel of God's promise of a posterity for Abraham. It is this allusion to resurrection, which cannot help but to recall to the minds of the audience the resurrection of Jesus, that we find the basis of the identification of human beings with Earth that gives rise to ecological response in the present.[19]

The term "resurrection" (*anastasis*) is infrequent in Hebrews, occurring three times. In 6:2, resurrection from the dead is listed as one of the foundational, basic teachings of Christ. The remaining two uses occur in

---

17. Ibid., 109, 139–42.
18. Buchanan, *Hebrews*, 72–74.
19. The author writes that "figuratively" Abraham did receive Isaac back from the dead. The Greek translated "figuratively" is *en parabolē*, and recalls the use of *parabolē* in 9:9, in which the earthly tabernacle is said to be a "parable" of the yet-to-be-revealed true tabernacle. So the term *parabolē* is used in 9:9 eschatologically. Craddock, *Hebrews*, 138–39, sees its use in 11:19 in a similar vein to point forward to both the resurrection of Jesus and all of God's faithful. Lane, *Hebrews 9–13*, 362–63, translates *en parabolē* with "in a foreshadowing" to highlight this understanding.

11:35, where women are said by faith to receive back their dead through resurrection and some refused deliverance to secure a better resurrection. So the three occurrences of the term all have in view the resurrection of human beings. The only explicit reference to the resurrection of Jesus occurs in the epistolary postscript in 13:20. However, a related tradition that appears to presuppose the resurrection of Jesus, the depiction of Jesus seated at the right hand of God, appears at least five times (1:3, 13; 8:1; 10:12; 12:2).[20] Clearly the priestly and sacrificial work of Jesus finds expression in Hebrews far more frequently and substantively than does the resurrection of Jesus. But the resurrection of Jesus is implicated in this priestly work of the Son via his enthronement at the right hand of God. The risen Jesus is the exalted Jesus who continues his priestly work of intercession at the right hand of God (7:25).

If the mention of the raising of the dead in 11:19 brings to mind the resurrection of Jesus, how precisely does this function as the point of identification of human beings with Earth? Earlier we argued that the author's description of the Son in 2:14 as one who became human, who took on flesh and blood, identifies the Son with human beings in his corporeality. But these same human beings are also connected to Earth via their creation from the dust of the ground (Gen 2:7). Using a variation on the transitive property, since the Son is connected to human beings by virtue of becoming human himself, and since human beings are connected to Earth by virtue of their creation from the stuff of Earth, then the Son is connected to Earth by virtue of sharing with human beings the stuff of Earth.[21] To use more theological language, the incarnation of the pre-existent and divine Son (cf. Heb 1:2–3a) is a strong affirmation of the goodness of creation.

However, our concern in the present discussion is not with creation, but with eschatology. So how does the resurrection of the incarnate Son identify us with Earth in such a way as to avoid the temptation of escapist eschatology to disregard the current condition of creation in favor of a state of eternal bliss? Here the work of N. T. Wright is indispensable. Wright follows up on his majesterial work on the resurrection, *The Resurrection of the Son of God*, with a more accessible volume, *Surprised by Hope*, in which he teases out the implications of the doctrine of the

20. 2:9 describes the Son as now crowned with glory and honor and may be an oblique reference to this tradition.

21. See ch. 2 above.

resurrection of Jesus for life in the present.[22] In Wright's famous idiom, God had done in the one man Jesus in the middle of time that which was expected for Israel at the end of time. As such, through the resurrection of Jesus the eschatological future has been brought back into the present time, bringing with it foretastes of that which awaits consummation on the last day. So the present order is seeded with those things that await it. In part and in increasing realization, the line from the Lord's Prayer finds fulfillment: "Your kingdom come. Your will be done, on earth as it is in heaven" (Matt 6:10).

In Wright's conception, the resurrection of Jesus anticipates the final coming together of heaven and earth in the end (cf. Rev 21–22). That which is identified with the present order, the incarnate Son, is raised from the dead, rescued from corruption, and glorified with heavenly glory as he is seated at the right hand of God. This point is crucial for Wright. Something of this present order has a place in heaven. But this is not a one-way transaction. The exalted Jesus is the currently reigning Lord over all creation, despite appearances to the contrary. And this Lord exercises his lordship through his presence among his people in the Holy Spirit and in the Eucharist. So something of heaven has a place in the present order. Moreover, those who have been baptized into his death and resurrection (cf. Rom 6) have been granted power through the indwelling Spirit to work toward the consummation of the kingdom of God, to embody, in a term appropriated from Crossan, "collaborative eschatology." Those so indwelt by the Spirit are themselves proleptic instantiations of the future kingdom in the present. In short, God's investment in the present order brought about by the resurrection of Jesus is indicative that God is not going to abandon the present creation to destruction.

Wright's project is far more extensive than this all too brief survey can justly describe, and much more could be said on the topics raised here and those left unmentioned. But we have said enough, I believe, to make an identification between human beings and Earth plausible. To sum up, the resurrection of Jesus is that which connects the present order to its redemption in the future. It does so by bringing together heaven and earth in the glorified man Jesus and through the encroachment of the coming kingdom into the present. But because human beings are connected to the man Jesus by virtue of shared humanity, which includes

---

22. The following discussion summarizes the argument of *Surprised by Hope*, especially chs. 3, 7–10, 13.

a shared connection with creation, human beings are further identified with an Earth that is not to be abandoned but is rather awaiting its full redemption in the future. The resurrection of Jesus is the point of contact that brings together human beings and Earth in an eschatological framework that does not abandon the present order to an inevitable doom, but rather gives place for Earth to speak to us about how we might evidence this eschatology in our present care for creation.

ECOLOGICAL EXPEDIENCE—HEARING THE VOICE OF EARTH

Hebrews 11:8–16 draws on the narrative of Abraham's sojourn to characterize the walk of faith that has its eyes set on the heavenly city as its ultimate inheritance. As we have seen, traditional interpretation of Hebrews has drawn the conclusion that the author of Hebrews is advocating an eschatology that is otherworldly, one that in its substance relativizes and in fact deprecates the place of the present created order in its pursuit of eternal reward. But we have observed in the author's continued appropriation of the Abraham narrative introduction of an idea through which we have observed a point of identification between human beings and Earth: resurrection. We noted that the resurrection of Jesus enables human identification with an Earth whose present order is continuous through redemption with the eschatological heavenly city of Heb 11:8–16. It remains to hear the voice of Earth in this construct.

There are two significant ways in which Earth might speak to us. The first is to show us that indeed the picture of Heb 11:8–16 is not incongruous with the eschatology put forth by Wright, and that it is within Hebrews itself that the balancing depiction is found. The second, and more important, message from Earth draws our attention to a different understanding of what is meant when Abraham is described in terms of the "resident alien." The first message is more theological, establishing the framework within which the more practical implications of the second message find expression.

First, Earth might remind us that the trajectory we called the "transience of the created order" may not be so firmly established as first thought. The final passage in that trajectory, 12:18–29, spoke of a "shaking" of heaven and earth that many commentators have argued results in the passing away of the created order. Some, however, question this outcome of the shaking. Lane notes that the shaking of heaven and earth is a recurring theme within pronouncements of the Day of the Lord (e.g., Isa 13:1–22; Hag 2:6; *Jub.* 1:29; 1 *En.* 45:1; *Sib. Or.* 3:675–80; 2 *Bar.* 32:1; 59:3), a metaphor of the judgment of God that is executed in history. The focus, in Lane's estimation, is not on the description of a future historical event that speaks to the temporal durability of the created order, but is rather a qualitative statement directed to survivability in the face of eschatological judgment.[23] Its use by the author of Hebrews is therefore not intended to speak about the destiny of creation, but rather to serve as a word of warning for readers to exhibit in their faithfulness those things that will endure in the face of judgment. "He concentrates his concern not on the future of the cosmos, but on the future of the new covenant community."[24] At this point, Laansma concurs and goes further. In his study of the cosmology of Hebrews, he argues that the author had in mind Ps 96 [95 LXX]:9 as he composed Heb 12:25–29. The two passages share significant vocabulary, particularly the language of "shaking," leading Laansma to the conclusion that what the author of Hebrews had in mind in appropriating the psalm was not the destruction of the cosmos, but rather the reclamation of the cosmos as God's temple through the removal of all that opposes God.[25] Focus on the possible transience of creation misses the point for which the passage was written.

Another detail in Heb 12:25–29 is frequently passed over without notice in these discussions. The word translated "removal," *metathesis*, is capable of another translation. Witherington notes that the term might also be translated "change" or "transformation," indicating that the material realm is not destined for removal, but rather is in store for "a sorting out and putting right," a transformation from the temporariness of the present order into the permanence of the future.[26]

In Heb 11:8–16, Abraham is depicted as seeking after a heavenly homeland, "a city that has foundations, whose architect and builder is God" (v. 10). Witherington sees in the terminology "architect" (*technitēs*) and "builder" (*dēmiourgos*) language used in Judaism to describe God's creation of the material world.[27] This leads Witherington to the conclu-

23. Lane, *Hebrews 9–13*, 480–83. So also O'Brien, *Hebrews*, 497–98.
24. Lane, *Hebrews 9–13*, 483.
25. J. Laansma, "Hidden Stories," 14.
26. Witherington, *Letters and Homilies*, 346.
27. Ibid., 309.

sion that the city is heavenly in its origin, but will become part of the transformed material realm at the eschaton. This is the meaning behind Heb 13:14: "For here we have no lasting city, but we are looking for the city that is to come" (cf. 2:5). The characterization of the city as that which is to come clearly has a temporal referent in view—it comes in the future; it may also have a locative referent as well—it comes to a renewed earth from heaven (cf. Rev 21:2, 10).[28]

So what is Earth's message to us in this lesson? It would be that the evidence from Hebrews itself is not so conclusive regarding interpretations that see it speaking of the elimination of the created realm from existence. Earth is not something from which human beings will escape in the eschaton. To be sure, Earth, like resurrected human beings, will exhibit remarkable transformation in God's promised future, but Earth, like humans, will remain. There is continuity between the present created order and the future dwelling place of human beings. The human connection with Earth will endure eternally.

The second way in which Earth speaks to human beings flows from the first. If human beings and Earth are inextricably connected both presently and eschatologically, if there is no escape from the material realm envisioned in God's future, how does this reality affect the present life of human beings on Earth? Here Earth reminds us of some implications of the characterization of Abraham as a "resident alien" in Heb 11:8–16. Interestingly, several commentators who focused on the otherworldliness of the patriarchs in the passage and the apparent transitoriness of creation also note that this does not preclude living beneficially in the present. Bruce notes that in the Genesis narratives, many around Abraham benefited from him,[29] while Koester notes that the future orientation displayed by Abraham should not lead to quietism and withdrawal, but to a life of service lived in light of the future.[30] These commentators evidence that a future orientation need not lead to the neglect of life in the present order.[31]

---

28. For a succinct discussion of the issues discussed here, see Adams, "Cosmology of Hebrews," 122–39.

29. Bruce, *Hebrews*, 300.

30. Koester, *Hebrews*, 498.

31. Lane, *Hebrews 9–13*, 359–60, notes the tension between future orientation and living in the present has ancient roots in Christian history. In *Diogn.* 5:9 Christians are described as those who live on earth but whose citizenship is in heaven (cf. 5:5–9), which

The "resident alien" is one whose citizenship lay elsewhere but who lives in someone else's territory. In his study of the biblical images of the land, Habel identifies one such image as the "immigrant ideology" of the Abraham narratives of Genesis. In this image, the land is seen as a host country where the immigrant ancestors of Israel sojourned as they discerned promises of a future homeland and in which they established peaceful relations with the indigenous peoples.[32] Here we see the joint foci of future orientation as well as connection with the present situation. Jewett understands this condition as the pilgrimage of a dialogue of faith with God, which in the context of Heb 11:8–16 he describes as follows: "To respond to that city is to take up the pilgrimage of dialogue that realistically accepts the finitude but never ceases to strive for the gradual though never final approximation of its qualities in whatever locale one happens to live."[33] This characterization again comes to grips with a desire to see the promise of the future come into the present in order to conform the conditions of present life more closely to the eschatological future. "Resident aliens" have a vested interest in the wellbeing of the community in which they dwell. As such, it behooves Christians as "resident aliens" in the present order to seek out the ecological wellbeing of Earth, both because it is beneficial for all in the present order and because it is a testimony of faith in the future that God has promised for the world.

The flipside of the theme of believers as "resident aliens" is that of Earth as a host country. In his ecological reading of Heb 11, Cadwallader draws attention to an intertextual echo in which the phrase "on the earth" in v. 13 replaces "in their land" from Gen 24:37. This change in language shifts focus from the narrow understanding of Canaan as a locale interested in the wellbeing of the seed of Abraham to a broad understanding of the whole world as being so concerned. In the context of Heb 11:8–16, then, the whole Earth is the city and homeland God grants to the people, and the adjectives "heavenly" and "better" describe a qualitatively different encounter with Earth.[34] An ecologically conscious response to Earth in the present demonstrates a sense of appreciation for the hospitality of Earth.

---

stands in stark contrast to the position articulated in Herm. *Sim.* 1:1, which castigates Christians for being too concerned with the things of this earth.

32. Habel, *Land*, ch. 7.

33. Jewett, *Letter to Pilgrims*, 205.

34. Cadwallader, "Earth as Host," 159–61.

This focus on the concept of the "resident alien" status of believers on Earth leads Earth to speak to us of the responsibility of these pilgrims to the wellbeing of the host country. Earth as host provides us with the resources for our survival as we await our future homeland. Earth calls us to work for its welfare, both because it benefits human beings and acknowledges that both we and Earth are destined for better things.

Maybe the way to distill the substance of Earth's voice in Heb 11:8–16 is to focus on the passage through an analogy. As the land traversed by Abraham later became the land of promise for Israel, perhaps we might see Earth as the land we traverse now that will also become our land of promise in the eschatological future. Earth asks, can life on Earth anticipate the coming heavenly city? Can the human exercise of ecological responsibility function sacramentally to point to the future restoration that awaits Earth? Can environmentally conscious practice be a present exercise of proleptic perfection? These are the questions Earth poses to us as we reflect on our relationship with Earth in light of Heb 11:8–16.

CONCLUSION

Hahne, in his study of the influence of Jewish apocalyptic on Paul's depiction of the future hope for the redemption of creation in Rom 8:19–22, has identified several strands of thought in apocalyptic literature regarding the destiny of the created order.[35] A large number of sources depict the future redemption of creation within two broad categories. One category sees the redemption of creation in terms of the removal of the current created order and its replacement with a new creation that is frequently described as existing in heaven and awaiting the people of God. As our study has shown, this is how the picture of Heb 11:8–16 is often understood, whether through the intent of the author of Hebrews or through the biases of subsequent interpreters.

The other category identified by Hahne sees the redemption of creation in terms of a renewal of the present order, frequently in terms of its transformation. Our study has shown that an ecological reading of Heb 11:8–16 that establishes an identification of human beings with the present created order via the resurrection of the Son enables us to hear the

---

35. Hahne, *Corruption and Redemption*. See the chart on p. 227 that summarizes the positions articulated in the examined sources of apocalyptic literature and how Paul's thought fits in with them.

voice of Earth in such a way as to live within and toward the continuity of the present order with its anticipated eschatological redemption. A reappraisal of the "resident alien" category coupled with Wright's conception of believers "building for the kingdom of God" provides the contours for living with a sense of ecological expedience in the present.

Our reading of this passage should not ultimately be seen as a reading in competition with the rhetorical interests of the author of Hebrews. The author's focus on the future hope for believers is wholly appropriate in the face of trials and persecutions that threaten to rob the original audience of this hope. In this respect, it would be unfair to critique our author for not explicitly addressing issues of concern for us in the process of addressing pressing issues for the first readers of Hebrews. At the same time, it would be equally unfair to press the rhetoric of the author to such a point as to eliminate the possibility for reading the text in other ways, especially when the cues for alternative readings are suggested in the same rhetoric. It is my hope that the present study has provided just such an alternative reading of Heb 11:8–16.

7

"We Have an Altar" (Hebrews 13:10)

The Reclamation of the Eucharist for Ecological Responsibility

INTRODUCTION

THE LETTER-SERMON OF HEBREWS has reinterpreted many symbols of the old covenant in light of the new covenant introduced through and by the Son. Many of these symbols have liturgical significance: Sabbath, sacrifice, priesthood, sanctuary, and various ablutions, to name some of the most prominent. What is more, many of these liturgically oriented symbols have established implicit connections between the worshiper and creation, concretizing in ritual observance the relationship between human beings and some aspect of the created order. However, in Hebrews, in each case, the symbol has been relativized through christological reinterpretation. In the process of reinterpretation, implicit connections between many of the cultic rituals and God's creation are lost, eroding the potential for concern for creation that might be reinforced through the performance of liturgical practice.

In Heb 13:10, the author makes mention of an altar from which no one who ministers under the old covenant has a right to eat. At this point, an original reader of this letter-sermon as well as a Christian reader from many traditions and periods in history might well have expected a reference to the Eucharist in connection with that altar. However, the subsequent discussion simply furthers the rhetorical strategy of the letter-sermon by connecting this altar with the sacrifice of Christ for the forgiveness of sins, suggesting that the proper worshipful response is to suffer with Christ outside the camp (v. 12), offer a sacrifice of praise that confesses the name of God (v. 15), and to share with others as a pleasing sacrifice to God (v. 16). What makes this significant is that through omission, either conscious or not, the author has diminished something within the Christian tradition that might have proven to be a useful point of identification between worshipers and creation, opting instead for the strategy of christological relativization that has characterized the entire argument. Up until now, the points of comparison have been between the Son and various elements of the old covenant; at this point, what may be present is an implicit comparison between two aspects of the new covenant—the Son who institutes it, and a liturgical practice within it. And again, the Son emerges superior.

Obviously, subsequent Christian history has shown the significant place the Eucharist has played in the worship life of various communions. However, this relativization through omission in Hebrews has also manifest in certain ecclesiastical traditions that are suspicious of and sometimes antagonistic to liturgical practice. And frequently, those traditions that minimize the more formal aspects of liturgical practice also follow the pattern of the author of Hebrews and "spiritualize" other aspects of the faith that would provide a valuable means of connection with creation.

This study will attempt to hear the voice of creation through an effort to reclaim one particular element of liturgical practice, namely, the Eucharist, as a point of connection between human beings and the created order. As we have seen previously, the author of Hebrews, perhaps unconsciously, has seeded the argumentation with a point of contact that allows for the appropriation of Eucharistic practice with the end in view of encouraging and enabling ecological responsibility fostered through faithful participation in the sacrament. Once again, the principles of ecological hermeneutics developed by the Consultation on Ecological Hermeneutics Section in the Society of Biblical Literature—suspicion, identification, retrieval—will form the shape of this study.

SUSPICION—A NON-EUCHARISTIC BIAS?

The assertion that the Eucharist plays a role in the care for creation will find defense in the next section of this study. For now, we will rest content with demonstrating that Hebrews depicts, within its rhetoric of relativizing and reinterpreting old covenant liturgical symbols in terms of the Son, a similar relativizing of the Eucharist in terms of the Son.

For our purposes, the crucial passage is Heb 13:10, which reads, "We have an altar from which those who officiate in the tent have no right to eat." This sentence follows on the exhortation of the previous verse not to follow after strange teachings but rather to be strengthened in the heart by grace. The author makes an apparent connection between these "strange teachings" and ineffectual food laws, suggesting, in light of the statement of v. 10, that the issue at hand may be the various ritual meals of the old covenant. This connection is perhaps strengthened by the mention in v. 11 that the bodies of animals sacrificed by priests were burned outside the camp, an observation that may elicit in the minds of readers the practice of priests eating the meat of certain sacrificed animals (e.g., Lev 7:6; Num 18:9-10).[1] But rather than identify the altar with the table of the Lord's Supper, the author goes on to speak of Jesus suffering outside the camp in order to sanctify the people (Heb 13:12) and to urge the readers to join in the abuse that Jesus suffered (v. 13), offering as they do the sacrifice of praise to God and the sacrifice of sharing their goods with one another (vv. 15-16). The flow of vv. 10-16 seems to suggest that whatever the precise identification of the altar in v. 10, it must somehow take into consideration Jesus and his sacrifice and actions from believers based on that sacrifice.

The issue of whether passages in Hebrews, such as 13:10 among others, point to endorsement of Eucharistic practice, has generated much debate among scholars, especially since the end of the nineteenth century. In a 1975 article, Williamson noted several scholars who held to the view that Hebrews makes reference in several passages, notably 13:10, to the Eucharist (e.g., Aalen, Moe, Andriessen), while others have argued that the Eucharist forms a dominant theme for the entire epistle (e.g., Field, Swetnam).[2] As Williamson has shown, scholars who identify certain passages as allusions to the Eucharist usually do so on the basis of certain vocabulary and conceptions, such as "flesh and blood" and "taste," that are too general or are too contextually connected to the author's rhetoric of

---

1. Buchanan, *Hebrews*, 234, suggests that such a connection between v. 11 and the eating of sacrificed meat by priests might be present; though Craddock, *Hebrews*, 166-67, notes that the sacrifices alluded to in v. 11 would not be permitted for priestly consumption.

2. See literature cited in Williamson, "Eucharist," 300-301. Williamson does not cite Thurén, *Das Lobopfer*, 83-91, 204, as one who holds that the Eucharist is the theme of Hebrews in its entirety. Swetnam, "Christology," 74-95.

speaking of the new covenant instituted by the sacrifice of Jesus to be explicitly identified with the Eucharist.³ That Hebrews does not make overt, explicit reference to the Eucharist is typically explained by noting that allusion is sufficient in light of the overarching thematic interests of the author in affirming the superiority of the new covenant instituted by the Son over against the institutions of the old covenant.⁴ Many more recent scholars have argued that the alleged allusions to the Eucharist in 13:10 are too tenuous onto which to stake a Eucharistic interpretation of the passage.⁵ Several lines of evidence are adduced. Those who do not see a Eucharistic intent here argue that the contextual evidence suggests seeing the altar as a symbol or metaphor for the sacrifice of Jesus for the forgiveness of sins. As noted above, v. 10 follows on v. 9, in which criticism is offered against food regulations that do not benefit those who eat accordingly. It would be an odd thing, in the minds of many, to turn around and advocate a new food regulation in the very next verse. Rather, the grace spoken of in v. 9 is effected in the new covenant through the suffering of Jesus (v. 12), access to which is denied those who labor under the regulations of the old covenant. Moreover, such an interpretation also makes sense in the larger context of the letter. Commentators have noted that the structure of the beginning of the verse—"we have an altar"—is similar to other confessions throughout the letter, suggesting that they have the same referent: a great high priest (4:14, 15; 8:1); hope as an anchor for the soul (6:19); confidence to enter the Most Holy Place (10:19).⁶ The parallel expressions link together 13:10 and its context with the argumentation developed elsewhere in the letter, thus cementing the notion that rather than speaking of the Eucharist, the author of Hebrews is simply reiterating what has gone before. Finally, as O'Brien notes, the nomenclature of "altar" is not widely used of the Lord's Supper until the second century, so such an allusion is not likely in 13:10.⁷ All of these considerations lead

---

3. Williamson, "Eucharist," 301–9.

4. Andriessen, "L'Eucharist," 269–77.

5. Attridge, *Hebrews*, 397; Bruce, *Hebrews*, 379–80; Craddock, *Hebrews*, 166–67; Ellingworth, *Hebrews*, 705–22; Johnson, *Hebrews*, 348–49; Koester, *Hebrews*, 568; Lane, *Hebrews 9–13*, 540; O'Brien, *Hebrews*, 521; Witherington, *Letters and Homilies*, 359–64.

6. Lane, *Hebrews 9–13*, 540; O'Brien, *Hebrews*, 521.

7. O'Brien, *Hebrews*, 521.

commentators to think that 13:10 does not refer to the Eucharist, even obliquely.[8]

Another group of scholars goes further than just suggesting that in 13:10—and in Hebrews in general—the author is not making reference to the Eucharist. Some see in the passage a virtually anti-Eucharistic sentiment present. Though not holding such a position himself, Bruce notes that had the Eucharist been in the author's mind at this point, it would have been an obvious context in which to make a direct connection, yet an explicit reference is missing.[9] So why is such a connection missing? Williamson, among others, suggests that it was because the Eucharist did not belong to the "beliefs and experience" of the author of Hebrews.[10] Williamson agrees with scholars before him who believed that Hebrews holds as one of its distinctive themes a view unlike many other NT writers, a view that sees the sacrifice of Christ not only rendering obsolete the rituals of the old covenant, but also rituals of any kind. There is therefore no need for any type of mediation between worshiper and God because of the grace evidenced in Christ's saving work. Again, such a view places the author and audience of Hebrews outside of the Eucharistic faith and practice of other early segments of the Jesus movement. As Williamson notes, given the polarity in the eschatology of Hebrews between the already and the not yet, had the community assumed by Hebrews practiced the Eucharist as part of its devotion, surely it would have been invoked as a sign of the foretaste of the heavenly bliss awaiting those who sojourn through this age in anticipation of "the city that has foundations, whose architect and builder is God" (11:10). And 13:10 would have been the perfect entrée into such a discussion. Its absence leads Williamson to conclude: "For the Christian, according to Hebrews, the Gospel always comes as a promise, to be received in faith; it can never be anticipated materially in a sacramental cultus."[11]

---

8. Bruce's words probably sum up the matter appropriately: "The most that can be said is that our author may be pointing to the truth of Christian experience which is independently attested in the Eucharist—that Christ is both the sacrifice and the sustenance of his people, and that as sacrifice and as sustenance alike he is to be appropriated by faith" (*Hebrews*, 380).

9. Bruce, *Hebrews*, 379–80.

10. Williamson, "Eucharist," 309. The following discussion summarizes 309–12.

11. Williamson, "Eucharist," 312.

If the absence of explicit mention of the Eucharist is too little on which to base the assumption of its presence, it is probably too little on which to base an assumed anti-sacramentalism.[12] Yet such a view has found currency in certain segments of Christian tradition. A latent anti-ritualism exists in some traditions, and in others the ritual is practiced without sacramental connotations. At some level, the attitude in such churches parallels what we see in the pages of Hebrews—an absence of the mention of the Eucharist in the devotional life of the respective communities.

At this point, we have simply shown that the Eucharist finds no explicit place in the argumentation of Hebrews, particularly in our passage of interest, 13:10. It has no place at all in the rhetorical strategy of the author. And we have observed that such a phenomenon has parallel at points in the subsequent tradition of the church. But does this constitute in any way an anthropocentric bias against the concerns of Earth? It does if it can be shown that the Eucharist in any way functions as a point of identification between human beings and Earth. So at least by virtue of the omission of the mention of the Eucharist from the argumentation of Hebrews, the author has removed from consideration an important point of contact between human beings and Earth, all in favor of the rhetorical interests of the author that, as we have seen, favor anthropocentric interests. The next step of our study will focus on establishing that the Eucharist is indeed a point of identification between human beings and Earth, as well as how Hebrews itself provides a way for reclaiming the Eucharist as this point of identification.

IDENTIFICATION—BREAD, WINE, AND EARTH

Exploring ecological connections with the practice and theology of the Eucharist is not an original idea, though it is an idea that is increasingly more popular in light of the ecological crises of the past half-century. Perhaps not surprisingly, it is more prevalent among Roman Catholic and Eastern Orthodox theologians.[13] For the purposes of the present discus-

---

12. So Craddock, *Hebrews*, 166–67.

13. Representative of Roman Catholic scholars is Edwards, *Ecology*, and of Orthodoxy Zizioulas, "Preserving God's Creation: Three Lectures on Ecology and Theology," 12:1–5, 41–45; and 13:1–5.

sion, we will focus on the identification forged in the recent work of Denis Edwards in his book, *Ecology at the Heart of Faith* (2006).[14]

Edwards develops a five-part model in which he attempts to construct an ecological theology of the Eucharist. The five parts do not appear to be a progression in the strict sense, but are rather more of a complex. First, the Eucharist is a lifting up of all creation to God. Here Edwards draws on the work of Zizioulas in the affirmation that human beings are truly human when they live as fully related, personal beings in communion with other human beings and with all creation. In this context, the Eucharist becomes a lifting up of creation, which is present in the elements of the Eucharist as the gifts of creation, in offering and thanksgiving to God. Such a view of the Eucharist creates an ecological ethos and culture with which to engage current ecological crises.

The second part of Edwards's model is that the Eucharist is a living memory of both creation and redemption. Not only is the Eucharist a living memory of what Christ has provided in redemption in the past, but it is also an active shaper of present living in anticipation of future life. But Edwards argues that more than simply redemption, important as it is, is implicit in the Eucharist. He notes that ancient Eucharistic prayers were based on Jewish prayers, especially those said at Passover, which begin with thanksgiving for creation before moving on to redemption. The presence of the creational motif in the Eucharist is evidenced in several places in the Eucharistic prayers of Roman Catholic liturgy. In the first Eucharistic prayer, thanksgiving is offered for the "fruit of the Earth and the work of human hands" in the provision of the elements. In the second prayer, Christ is lauded as "the Word through whom [God] made the universe, the Savior you sent to redeem us," drawing together both the creation and redemption motifs in the Eucharist. In the third and fourth prayers, the notion of the praise of creation is present: "All creation rightly gives you praise" and "In the name of every creature under heaven, we too praise your glory," respectively. In each of these instances, Earth and human beings are drawn together in the Eucharist through the joint foci of creation and redemption.

The third aspect of Edwards's model is what he calls the sacrament of the cosmic Christ. In the Eucharist, as worshipers celebrate the redemption provided by Christ, they celebrate the one who achieved this

14. The following discussion summarizes Edwards, *Ecology*, 99–108.

redemption by handing his bodily and personal existence over to a loving God. Recall, this is the same Christ who as the eternal Son was the agency through which God brought all things into being (cf. Col 1:15–20; Heb 1:2–3a). The cosmic Christ is the embodied Christ. And following the death of the embodied Christ, he was resurrected and seated in heaven. Here, a citizen of the very universe he created was taken up into the Spirit of God, marking the beginning of new creation. The Eucharist is the sacrament of the risen Christ, who is the beginning of the transformation of the whole cosmos. So all creation is now the place of encounter with the risen Christ, who is identified in the Eucharist with the bread and wine, the produce of Earth. The Eucharist becomes a means by which human beings encounter the cosmic Christ who identifies himself with creation through the bread and wine.

The fourth plank of Edwards's approach is the Eucharist as a participation with all of God's creatures in the communion of the Trinity. The Eucharist is both a Trinitarian and an eschatological event. As such, it moves participants toward the time when all things will be taken up into the eternal life of the Trinity. Moreover, since all life proceeds from the creative act of the Triune God, the Eucharist serves as the bond of the community of all life as brought forth by the Trinity. The Eucharist is not simply the communion of human beings with God; it is the communion of all of God's creation with God.

The final aspect of Edwards's model of an ecological Eucharist is its solidarity with the victims of ecological degradation. The Eucharist by its very nature involves memory of the cross. This memory stands as a challenge to complacency in the face of the sufferings of others. Environmental degradation disproportionately affects the global poor. So as worshipers around the world celebrate the Eucharist, as living memory it draws them to the cross in solidarity for all objects of God's redemption who suffer the ills of ecological disaster.

In this sketch of an ecological Eucharist, Edwards has demonstrated that the Eucharist serves as a viable point of identification between human beings and Earth. What remains is to determine if this Eucharistic point of identification actually serves us in any way with respect to Hebrews. To this we now turn our attention, directing our focus to a passage six chapters earlier than our text of choice, to the enigmatic figure of Melchizedek.

The figure of Melchizedek appears in only two places in the Hebrew Bible, Gen 14:18–20 and Ps 110:4. The latter passage, which refers to a priesthood established according to the order of Melchizedek, figures significantly into the christological argument of Hebrews, quoted in 5:6 and 7:17, with further allusions to the priesthood along Melchizedek's order occurring four more times (5:10; 6:20; 7:11, 15). Hebrews 7 is the place where Melchizedek figures prominently into the argument, with the author drawing on the citation from Ps 110 to establish both the necessity of this new order of priesthood and its eternality. But for our purposes, the discussion of Heb 7:1–10 is more pertinent, as it focuses primarily on the author's creative appropriation of the primary OT reference to Melchizedek, Gen 14:18–20.

The Melchizedek account occurs in the midst of the story of Abram returning from his defeat of Chedorlaomer and those kings who fought with him (14:17) in which he rescued his kidnapped nephew Lot, and Abram's subsequent meeting with the king of Sodom in the Valley of Shaveh. The account is short and worth quoting in full:

> And King Melchizedek of Salem brought out bread and wine; he was priest of God Most High. He blessed him and said,
> "Blessed be Abram by God Most High, maker of heaven and earth; and blessed be God Most High, who has delivered your enemies into your hand!"
> And Abram gave him one tenth of everything.

From here, Melchizedek disappears from the pages of the Hebrew Bible until his mention in Ps 110. But this brief episode provides the fodder for the author of Hebrews to begin the crucial exposition of the superior priesthood of the Son.

The author's exposition of Melchizedek begins with a selective appropriation of the details of the story, effectively summarizing the story in the opening lines of the passage (vv. 1–2a). Notably missing from the author's introduction of Melchizedek in the Genesis account is the mention of bread and wine. But also missing is the content of Melchizedek's blessing of Abram, which makes mention of the Most High as "maker of heaven and earth." As we noted above, the line "maker of heaven and earth" recalls the Passover prayers that lay behind the Eucharistic prayers of the early Christians. In the author's selectivity, we perhaps witness again a bias of omission against the ritual practice of the Eucharist. Rather, what we do see is an etymology lesson that plays off the name "Melchizedek" and his city of residence, "Salem." His identification as the king of righteousness and peace is certainly meant to evoke their recognition in the Son, yet the author does not make much mileage from this. Instead, the author points to a detail missing from the Genesis account, namely, the absence of a genealogy. Most commentators recognize here that the author is making a literary observation about Melchizedek, not an ontological one.[15] The absence of a genealogy, the lack of mention of father and mother, is employed to show that he has no point of origin in terms of birth. Nor is there mention of his death. Thus he is without beginning or end, in other words, eternal, occupying an eternal order in semblance with the Son of God (v. 3).

Beginning with v. 4, the author engages in a more extended discussion that derives from another detail drawn from the Genesis account: Abram's payment of a tithe to Melchizedek. The author's point is that because of the lineage of Abram that eventually produces Levi, in effect Levi paid the tithe to Melchizedek through Abram, indicating to our author that the priesthood of Levi is illustrated as inferior to that of Melchizedek by virtue of the direction of payment. And since the priesthood of the Son is along the lines of that of Melchizedek, by inference the priesthood of the Son is superior to that of the Levitical priesthood. The facts and arguments of Heb 7:1–10 then provide the launching pad for the more extended discussion of the Son's priesthood in the remainder of ch. 7.

As is evident, the author's selective use of the scant biblical Melchizedek tradition serves his own christological agenda. Here we see again evidence of bias, and we might well have discussed this above when discussing the authors' biases against Earth. But in Melchizedek we see a point of identification. Surely in such a short story the audience would be familiar enough with Melchizedek not only to recognize what the author chose to include, but also to recognize what the author chose to exclude. At the very least, subsequent generations of interpreters would recognize this. And indeed, very early interpreters saw this omission and addressed it. Several patristic sources have seen in the Melchizedek account in Genesis a prefiguring of the Eucharistic meal, particularly in the priestly ministry of Christ and extending through to the priestly ministry of the church.[16] The image of the bread and wine in Melchizedek's blessing of Abram coupled with the mention of the Most High God as "maker of

---

15. E.g., Bruce, *Hebrews*, 159–60; Craddock, *Hebrews*, 86; O'Brien, *Hebrews*, 248–50.

16. E.g., Eusebius of Caesarea, *Proof of the Gospel* 5:3; Cyprian, *Letter* 62:4; Epiphanus of Salamis, *Panarion* 4, *Against Melchizedekians* 6:1–11; Clement of Alexandria, *Stromateis* 4:25; Jerome, *Hebrew Questions on Genesis* 14:18–19.

heaven and earth" brings together both the Eucharistic and the creational motifs that we saw above in Edwards's thinking.

So the biblical Melchizedek tradition in its selective use by the author of Hebrews to buttress the rhetorical strategy of the argumentation turns out not to be able to mask a point of identification with Earth. As Edwards has shown, the Eucharist, replete with creational motifs, forges a powerful connection between human worshipers and Earth. And the tradition of Melchizedek, despite the creative use of it engineered by the author of Hebrews, interjects images that unavoidably bring to mind the Eucharist, and for ecologically oriented readers, a point of identification with Earth. So whether the author simply omits reference to the Eucharist either in ch. 7 or in 13:10 for rhetorical or strategic reasons, or whether he consciously omits such reference out of an anti-Eucharistic motivation, the Melchizedek tradition so skillfully employed forces the Eucharist into consideration in the minds of a church so powerfully shaped by Eucharistic devotion. In the final section of this discussion, we will look at how this Eucharistic point of identification introduced by the author's use of the Melchizedek tradition empowers Earth to speak on its own behalf.

RETRIEVAL—EARTH'S CALL FOR EUCHARISTIC RENEWAL

So in light of the aforementioned biases and the point of identification between human beings and Earth in the Eucharist, what might the voice of Earth articulate for those who read Heb 13:10 from an ecological vantage point? After all, at the very least, the author of Hebrews has effectively excluded Eucharistic implications from consideration; at most, the author has indicated an anti-Eucharistic bias through omission of its mention in places where such mention might have actually contributed to the author's argumentation. The course of the present discussion has brought us to the figure of Melchizedek, excavating from the biblical Melchizedek tradition a connection to the Eucharist that brings human beings to identification with Earth. Now at this point, we suggest two issues Earth might bring to our awareness as we seek to hear Earth's voice call out for human ecological responsibility in our practice of Eucharistic devotion.

First, Earth might suggest to us that we look beyond what a more traditional historical-critical exegesis of Heb 13:10 yields in terms of original meaning to how this verse has informed and influenced the faith and practice of the church throughout history. Here the work of Ulrich Luz is instructive. Building upon the work of Gadamer, Luz has developed a methodological approach to reading Scripture known as the "history of effects" (*Wirkungsgeschichte*).[17] This approach seeks both to observe how a biblical text has exerted influence in the church through history as well as to interpret Scripture so as to appropriate the biblical texts in an ongoing, powerful way in conversation with the changing situations that confront the church as the church lives in and engages the world. Said another way, the history of effects approach to reading the Bible allows for the text to connect with readers intentionally in such a way that appreciates the context of the reader in both the church and the world.

So how does the history of effects approach inform an ecological reading of Heb 13:10? It acknowledges, first, that the author of Hebrews had a particular agenda in mind with respect to whatever exigence gave rise to the rhetoric and argumentational strategies in the letter. With respect to the possible association of Eucharist and altar in 13:10, it candidly admits that the author chose, for whatever reason, not to make an appeal to the Eucharist at this point. But this approach also notes that relatively soon in church history, the image of the altar and the practice of the Eucharist would come together, and that such a connection would seem natural to readers who worshiped in traditions where Eucharist and altar occupied the same conceptual space. This would be particularly true given that the mention of the altar in connection with the sacrifice of Jesus in the larger context of 13:9–16 draws together the images of altar and sacrifice in the concrete liturgical practice of followers of Jesus, both early in the history of the movement as well as among a significant segment of the movement throughout history. This is also true given that the language of 13:9–16 occurs under the long shadow cast by the author's use of the Melchizedek tradition in which several patristic commentators saw the foreshadowing of the Eucharistic meal in the portion omitted by the author of Hebrews. In short, it would be quite natural for a worshiping community formed around Eucharistic practice to see allusions to the meal in the author's altar imagery of 13:10 in light of subsequent Christian interpretation of Melchizedek traditions that see beyond the author's treatment of Melchizedek.

In short, Earth might suggest to the Eucharistic community that it read Heb 13:10, not primarily through the eyes of a historical-critical

17. Luz, *Matthew in History*.

approach that sheds insight into what the author was trying to communicate through the chosen rhetoric and argumentation within a particular historical exigence, but also to read the passage through the eyes of how the church had come to associate the image of the altar with the practice of the Eucharist. Moreover, the author's use of the figure of Melchizedek, who had come to be viewed by early interpreters as one who had prefigured the Eucharist in his service of the bread and wine to Abram, further invites a Eucharistic connection with the image of the altar in 13:10 in the imagination of Christian interpreters. Where the author had not made direct appropriation of the Eucharist in the argumentation of Hebrews, subsequent interpreters may make such appropriation as they read Hebrews through the "Eucharistic eyes" of its identity as a Eucharistic people.

At this point, however, Earth would quickly point out that simply seeing the Eucharist here is not adequate to inculcate ecological responsibility in those who participate in Eucharistic celebration. Here we are introduced to the second thing Earth might suggest as we seek to hear its voice in Heb 13:10. Earth might say to us that we need to integrate a more conscious identification with Earth in our practice of Eucharistic devotion, with the result that such an identification might shape a more robust ecological awareness as part of a Eucharistically-shaped life in the world. We have already noted above how the Eucharist forges an identification between Earth and human worshipers. What Earth here suggests is moving beyond the grounds for making such an identification to the integration of these grounds into both liturgical practice and living in the world.

Here again we return to the work of Edwards. Earlier we noted how Edwards sought to construct an ecological theology of the Eucharist. In this attempt, we saw how the Eucharist forges an identity between human beings and Earth. Following his sketch of an ecological theology of the Eucharist, he provides some suggestions as to how this theology works out in terms of spirituality and practice.[18] In short, what Edwards describes is what he calls an ecological conversion through the celebration of the Eucharist. There are three elements to his proposal.

The first he calls the "Way of Wisdom." This aspect is described as a following of Jesus Christ, who is the embodied Wisdom of God, in the way of wisdom. This way of wisdom involves a loving respect for all of God's creatures, evoking an enlightenment that bears fruit in our engage-

---

18. Edwards, *Ecology*, 108–18. The following summarizes his discussion.

ment with creation. It is a cultivation of a loving eye that sees all aspects of God's creation as expressions of divine wisdom. Recall that in his ecological theology of the Eucharist, Edwards described how the Eucharist was a sacrament of the cosmic Christ, one who was involved in the creation of the cosmos. As we noted in an earlier chapter,[19] the Son is depicted in terms of wisdom in his creating and sustaining roles with respect to the cosmos. In the celebration of the Eucharist, we celebrate the one who is God's Wisdom and who ordered and sustains all things according to this divine wisdom. This celebration then opens our eyes to walk daily in accordance with the Wisdom and the wisdom by which all things express God's wisdom.

Edwards calls the second element of his proposal "Praxis in the Spirit." Again, Jesus is the exemplar of this aspect. What Edwards calls for is a praxis, consisting of both reflection and action, that is led by the Holy Spirit as was Jesus. Edwards casts this largely as a Spirit-led expansion of our moral vision that takes in life in communion with all of creation. At the center of this Spirit-led praxis is celebration, particularly the celebration of the Eucharist. This aspect of Edward's spirituality and practice draws heavily from his theological construction, particularly from his understanding of the Eucharist as a Trinitarian event that draws all of God's creation, human and other than human, into the communion of Trinitarian life. And deriving from this communion is the responsibility to live as a witnessing, or martyr, church, giving voice to the voiceless.

The third element of Edwards's proposal is called "Mysticism of Ecological Praxis." In many ways, this element serves as a summary, or perhaps better a consequence, of the previous two elements. In short, it simply urges a view toward life that emphasizes the communion of being in the world, living in light of all that is entailed in the ecological theology of the Eucharist. It is a mysticism of everyday living, a joining together of prayer and action. The identification of human beings and Earth enacted in the Eucharistic celebration shapes the moral imagination of worshipers and fuels a response of prayer and action that issues forth in concrete expressions of ecological praxis.

These two aspects of Earth's voice perhaps have in view two different segments within the church. The first may speak to those groups who follow the pattern of the author of Hebrews, those who either marginalize

---

19. See ch. 2 above.

the significance of the Eucharist or who may exhibit some type of opposition to its practice. The call of Earth is then to look beyond what the author of Hebrews does and to expand the vision of their own devotion. The second aspect speaks to those who have a significantly high view of the Eucharist in their worship. The call of Earth here is to expand the vision of what that devotion entails for Earth. The prospect of the first aspect achieving success among those for whom the Eucharist has marginal significance is probably not very great. The greater hope is that Earth finds a receptive audience in the second group. In either instance, the Eucharist offers a liturgical and practical point of contact through which to hear the voice of Earth.

CONCLUSION

As we have seen in the previous studies in this volume, the author of Hebrews, for reasons germane to the rhetoric of the letter-sermon, exhibits a bias against Earth in the exposition of the argumentation. In this instance, it was more of a bias of indirection. We started with the observation that the author had omitted reference to the Eucharist in contexts where appeal to it might have strengthened the argument. In this omission, the author has effectively eliminated from consideration one aspect of Christian worship that, as we showed in the section on identification, establishes a connection between human beings and Earth, all in favor of the more anthropocentrically weighted agenda of Hebrews. So a bias against the Eucharist is in effect a bias against Earth. But with the identification of human beings with Earth forged by the Eucharist, Earth calls out to participants in the sacrament to read in 13:10, and in the edited Melchizedek tradition to which the author appeals, a summon to expand the vision of Eucharistic devotion to motivate a praxis of ecological responsibility in the world.

Reading Hebrews has led many to relativize the necessity and significance of liturgical practice for the church. At the very least, Hebrews seems to reinterpret and relocate many old covenant rituals in the Son, which has had the effect, intended or otherwise, of diminishing the importance of the actual rituals themselves. Nevertheless, as we have seen numerous times in our studies, the author of Hebrews has left the door open, perhaps inadvertently, for interjection of considerations that lend themselves to an ecological reading of the letter. Such is what we argued here with respect to the Eucharist, in hope that the words "we have an altar" rise above the merely indicative to the effect of an imperative.[20]

---

20. Much the same might have been argued with respect to baptism as a point of identification with Earth. In Heb 9:10, the author denigrates Jewish washing rituals as ineffective. Yet in 6:2, teaching concerning "baptisms" is identified as part of the foundational teaching for which the readers are chided for not having matured beyond. Given the complex of ideas present in the context (vv. 1–5)—repentance, faith, baptisms, laying on of hands, enlightenment, Holy Spirit, powers of the age to come—some have suggested that Christian baptism is in view here (e.g., Ellingworth, *Hebrews*, 316; Johnson, *Hebrews*, 159; Koester, *Hebrews*, 305–11). An ecological reading of these texts would demonstrate that baptism, like the Eucharist, is a point of identification between human beings and Earth, and then proceed to follow Luz's methodology to read 6:2 in light of the history of effects to retrieve Earth's voice along the lines of a praxis of new life for the baptized community in the world.

8

Creational Christology Redux

Angels, Torah, Son, and Creation (Hebrews 2:1–4)

INTRODUCTION

WITH THIS STUDY WE come full circle, returning to the topic with which we began. "Creational christology" is the label we gave to a trajectory of passages, including Heb 1:2–3a, that speaks of the agency of Christ in the creation of the cosmos. In that initial study, we observed that the author of Hebrews employed the motif of the creative agency of the Son for the purposes of the argument of the letter-sermon. The creative agency of the Son was not a topic that merited its own consideration, but rather served the argument of the author, namely, to demonstrate the superiority of the Son over against various aspects of the old covenant. In that study, we employed an ecological reading of the passage in its context that allowed us to hear the voice of Earth in a passage in which such was not the concern of the author.

In the present study, we will again focus on the christology of the author in a creational context, but do so in a passage that might not at first glance seem to have the creative agency of the Son in view. Hebrews 2:1–4 serves as the second half of an *inclusio* for the discussion that began with 1:1–4 and in which the revelation of God given under the old covenant is brought into connection with angels and found inferior by comparison with the revelation of God that is the Son. As noted, appeal to the creative agency of the Son is explicit in the opening paragraph of Hebrews. How might we see a similar focus in 2:1–4 where such an appeal is clearly not explicit?

This study will examine 2:1–4 in its context as the climax of the argument of Hebrews to this point in the letter-sermon. The discussion will attempt to show that in its own idiom the creative agency of the Son is present in a way that somewhat parallels the conceptual framework that lies behind the explicit assertion of creative agency in 1:2–3a. As such, the paragraph 2:1–4 forms a fitting conclusion to the strand of argumentation in this section of Hebrews, and in the context of an ecological reading of the passage, solidifies the conclusions we drew in our study of 1:2–3a earlier in this volume. Again, we will employ the criteria of suspicion, identification, and retrieval in this study, though we will not duplicate assertions from the first study that will be equally valid in the present study.

SUSPICION—THE SUPERIORITY OF THE SON TO TORAH

Hebrews begins, not with the salutation typical of NT letters, but with the assertion that God in the past had spoken in many diverse ways through numerous prophets (1:1). No sooner had the author affirmed the revelatory word of God in the past, he goes on to assert that this revelation has been surpassed through revelation by a Son, one who is described as creator, heir, and sustainer of all things, one who reflects the glory of God and who is the exact imprint of God's very being, one who made purification for sins and now sits at the right hand of God (vv. 2–3).[1] Given this comparison between the prophets and the Son as conduits of God's revelation, the conclusion arrived at in v. 4 comes as somewhat of a surprise: the Son's name is superior to that of the angels. The subsequent exegesis of the catena of OT passages in vv. 5–14 proves the point of v. 4, at least as far as the author is concerned, namely, of the Son's superiority over angels. It is not until 2:1–4 that readers are let in on the reason for the sudden shift from prophets to angels back in 1:4: the demonstration of the Son's superiority over angels serves to illustrate the point of 1:1–3, the superiority of the revelation of the Son over against the revelation given through the prophets. The point is that the very revelation described as given through prophets in 1:1 is the message declared through angels in 2:2.[2] Of course, the revelation through the Son (1:2) is superior to that of

---

1. Attridge, *Hebrews*, 37, contends that the multiplicity and diversity of revelation spoken through the prophets is surpassed by the singular and thus final revelation in the Son. Cf. O'Brien, *Hebrews*, 49.

2. Lane, *Hebrews 1–8*, 18, argues that the mention of angels in 1:4 serves as a counterpart to the mention of prophets in v. 1. Though he is correct, his line of argumentation

the prophets, and the message spoken through the Lord (2:3) is superior to the message declared through angels.

What makes this connection possible is the author's mention of the tradition that the pinnacle of the old covenant revelation, the Torah given through Moses, the chief of the prophets of old, was mediated through angels. While the role of angels in mediating Torah is not found in the account of Exod 19 and 20, in Deut 33:2 Moses declares that God came to Sinai with "myriads of holy ones."[3] By the first century CE, this tradition was widely attested in Second Temple Jewish sources (*Jub.* 1:27; 2:1, 26–27; CD 5:18), in the NT (Acts 7:38, 53; Gal 3:19), and in Josephus (*Ant.* 15:5:3; 15:36), and was apparently shared by the author and readers of Hebrews.[4] Having given extensive scriptural proof that the Son is superior to the angels (1:5–13), the connection of angels to the transmission of Torah, the most significant aspect of the revelation given through the prophets, cements the initial contention of the author that the revelation of the Son is superior to the revelation given through the prophets.

So the revelation through the Son is superior to the revelation of the old covenant, a result confirmed in large part by the demonstration of the Son's superiority to angels. How does this constitute a bias against Earth? At one level, we might again note that the very fact that the author chose to pursue a christological rather than a creational agenda in this part of the letter-sermon is at least an implicit bias against Earth, one that does have beneficial ramifications for human beings. But the pursuit of this agenda in 1:1—2:4 produces two more definitive biases against Earth, one in the catena that demonstrates the superiority of the Son over angels and one in the statement that the revelation spoken through the Lord is superior to the message declared by angels (2:2–3).

The catena of 1:5–14 begins with the establishment of the superior status of the Son by virtue of his position as a son. The author begins in v. 5 by framing a question, "to which of the angels did God ever say," completing this clause with two scriptural citations, Ps 2:7 and 1 Sam 7:14. The obvious response is, "to none of them."[5] The author then de-

---

requires the development of the rhetoric culminating in 2:1–4 to substantiate his point. It is not explicitly apparent in 1:4 that the introduction of angels into the argument confirms the contrast made in 1:1–3.

3. The LXX reads "angels were with him at his right hand."

4. Lane, *Hebrews* 1–8, 18.

5. Ellingworth, *Hebrews*, 110; and O'Brien, *Hebrews*, 66, note that the rhetorical ques-

clares the hierarchical relationship between angels and the Son in v. 6, when he draws on the language of Deut 32:43 and of Ps 97 [96 LXX]:7 to indicate that the angels are called to worship the Son.[6] But in vv. 7–12 we come to the portion of the catena that is most pertinent for our purposes. In v. 7, the author cites Ps 104 [103 LXX]:4 to speak of the transitory nature of angels in their ministrations in the cosmos. The Hebrew text of the verse spoke of God making the winds his messengers and flames of fire his servants. The Greek text, however, reverses the objects and thus speaks of angels in terms of their transitory nature, fleeting as the winds and flames of fire.[7] The transitory nature of angels is contrasted with the eternal nature of the Son in vv. 8–9. The author cites Ps 45:6–7 [44:7–8 LXX] to indicate that the Son, addressed by God with the vocative, "O God," is superior to angels precisely because he is divine. The translation of the first line of the citation has occasioned much debate, though the traditional rendering, "Your throne, O God, is forever and ever," has been ably defended by Harris,[8] and fits well with the context of the catena. Its placement here identifies the Son as one who is eternal (1:8–9), worthy of the worship of angels (1:6) by virtue of the fact that the Son is the divine creator of all things (1:10; cf. 1:2–3), including the angels themselves. This line of argumentation culminates in vv. 10–12, where the author cites Ps 102:25–27 [101:26–28 LXX] to argue further that the Son is eternal. Taken in conjunction with the previous quotation in vv. 8–9, the sequence begins and ends with strong affirmations of the Son's eternality (vv. 8, 12). This affirmation contrasts vividly with the mutability of the angels described earlier in the passage (v. 7).[9] The catena closes in v. 13 in parallel structure with v. 5. The author again frames a question, "to which of the angels did God ever say," followed by the scriptural citation of Ps 110:1. The questions in both v. 5 and v. 13 draw on Davidic

---

tion functions as equivalent to an emphatic negation, drawing on the work of Beekman and Callow, *Translating*, 229–48.

6. The Septuagintal language of the psalm was probably chosen because it explicitly mentions angels and thus serves the subordinating interests of the author more clearly. So Lane, *Hebrews 1-8*, 28; O'Brien, *Hebrews*, 70–71.

7. O'Brien, *Hebrews*, 71.

8. Harris, *Jesus as God*, 187–227. Harris surveys the possible translations of the line and concludes that it makes the most sense of the syntax and also of its placement in the argument of Heb 1:5–14.

9. Lane, *Hebrews 1-8*, 30–31; O'Brien, *Hebrews*, 75.

enthronement psalms to frame the discussion of the Son's superiority over angels by casting the argument in terms of the Son's exalted position of glory and honor over all aspects of creation, including angels.[10] The series of scriptural citations is concluded in v. 14 with another question that asserts that angels are "spirits in the divine service" sent to minister to those who will inherit salvation.[11] This ascription of angels recalls the language of Ps 104:4 cited in v. 7, cementing the notion that angels are subordinated to the Son and serve him as he identifies with human beings as he brings them to glory (cf. 2:10).[12]

So how does this passage indicate a bias against Earth? The passage is intent on demonstrating that the Son is superior to the angels, and a significant part of that argumentation had to do with a contrast of the transitory nature of angels with the eternal nature of the Son. But a close look at one of the scriptural citations employed in this argument, Ps 102:25–27 in vv. 10–12, draws a further contrast, one between the transitory nature of the created order with the eternal nature of the Son. The net effect of this pair of contrasts draws Earth into the company of angels. This "guilt by association" relegates Earth to a subordinate position with respect to the Son. Clearly the author of Hebrews, as well as most in Jewish and Christian traditions, would acknowledge as an article of faith that the creator is exalted over the creature. However, as we saw in an earlier discussion, the citation of this psalm in vv. 10–12 has frequently been used to argue for an "escapist eschatology" that denigrates the place of Earth in the economy of redemption.[13] It is not the subordination per se that is at issue; the evaluation of the subordination frequently is. At the very least, consideration of Earth as an entity of intrinsic worth and consideration in itself is a casualty of the author's concern to demonstrate the superiority of the Son over angels precisely at the point of the transitory nature of angels and Earth. The Son is superior to the angels because he is their creator; the same holds true for Earth. So in the final analysis, while it is clearly a datum of Jewish and Christian ontology that this should be so, the rhetorical strategy of the author of Hebrews, in its use of this fact,

---

10. Attridge, *Hebrews*, 62; Lane, *Hebrews 1–8*, 32; O'Brien, *Hebrews*, 77.

11. The Greek here is *leitourgika pneumata*; in v. 7, *pneumata* (translated there "winds") and *leitourgous* (translated there "servants").

12. Bruce, *Hebrews*, 65; O'Brien, *Hebrews*, 79.

13. See ch. 6 above.

is biased against Earth as it argues full bore for the superiority of the Son over angels.

We also observe the author's bias against Earth as we examine the culmination of this section of the argument in 2:1–4. As we have noted, the demonstration of the Son's superiority over the angels serves another purpose, namely, to demonstrate the superiority of the revelation in the Son over the revelation mediated through angels, the Torah. So how does the Son's superiority over Torah betray a bias against Earth? In Second Temple Judaism, eventually the wisdom to which was ascribed creative agency in the Hebrew Bible had come to be identified with Torah (Sir 24:23; 33:3; 39:1; Bar 3:15-4:1; 4 Macc 1:16-17).[14] This identification had two effects. First, it particularized what was earlier a more universalizing tendency of wisdom, effectively restricting wisdom and its pursuit with the study of Torah. Secondly, whereas in earlier Hebrew wisdom traditions Yahweh's wisdom served as the pattern for the construction of the cosmos, Torah had become the template for creation (*Pirqe 'Abot* 3:23; Philo, *Creation* 3).[15] So not only do the angels have a connection with Earth, so too does Torah, and as we have seen with respect to the angelic connection with Earth, guilt by association with something demonstrated as inferior with respect to the Son renders Earth as inferior to the Son. And while such a conclusion is quite natural in the theological context of Hebrews, it has the effect of rendering null any possibility of considering Earth as an agenda of merit in light of the rhetorical aims of the author. A similar effect is implicit in the comparison of Torah with the Son.

While admittedly this latter bias is much more weakly attested than that connected with the comparison of the Son with angels, it is implicit within the flow of the argument. Its primary value, however, lay in its role in providing a point of identification with Earth. To this we now turn our attention.

IDENTIFICATION—ANOTHER FORAY INTO WISDOM

In ch. 2, we identified a point through which the voice of Earth might be retrieved in the very christology employed by the author. Linguistic links between the attributes predicated of the Son in 1:2-3a and those predicated of wisdom in Wisd 7:22-8:1 allowed us to hear Earth call hu-

---

14. See discussion in Lamp, *First Corinthians* 1–4, 27–29.
15. Gaston, *Paul*, 23–27.

man beings to the recognition of the Son's presence in the created order. So how does this help us to see an identification with Earth?

As we noted above, in the Judaism of the Second Temple period wisdom had come to be identified with Torah. Hebrews 2:1–4 has brought the argumentation of this section of the letter-sermon to a point of comparison in which the revelation in the Son is superior to the revelation through Torah. Both the Son and Torah are the embodiments of divine revelation in their respective covenantal contexts. At this level of the comparison, the focus is more on their direct revelatory expressions. Torah, whether understood in terms of the written or oral traditions, is largely an encoded revelation, represented linguistically. The Son, by contrast, is the living icon of the invisible God. As such, the revelation in the Son surpasses the revelation mediated through the angels, in a comparison that resembles strategically Paul's argument in 2 Cor 3:2–3. A living revelation surpasses a written one. So at the level of the direct substantial expression of the revelation, the Son surpasses Torah. It is this focus on the direct revelation of Son and Torah through which the author of Hebrews establishes the superiority of the Son over Torah.

The point of identification of human beings with Earth comes at the level of indirect revelation. As we noted in ch. 2 above, wisdom functions to bring together Earth and human beings. We also noted in that discussion that through the Son's human embodiment, human beings are connected to the Earth created through the Son. And we also saw that the Son is identified with this divine wisdom. The triad humanity-Son-Earth exhibits the strong interconnections between human beings and Earth, with wisdom functioning as a sort of conceptual cement that connects the pieces. Having established that the Son's revelation is superior to Torah's, Heb 2:1–4 provides a framework for assessing the superiority of the Son over Torah in other arenas. Wisdom had come to be identified with Torah; for the writer of Hebrews, wisdom is identified with the Son, an identification present in other segments of the fledgling Christian movement.[16] So an extension of the logic of the comparison in this passage suggests that the Son is a superior wisdom to that of Torah.

As a superior wisdom, the Son provides the proper channel for engaging Earth for what Earth might tell us about God. If the Son is the wisdom of God, the one through whom God ordered the cosmos, then

---

16. Cf. Lamp, *First Corinthians* 1–4, ch. 5.

the study of the created order should provide insight into the God who so ordered the universe through the Son. This more indirect mode of revelation, again, is not explicitly the concern of the author. However, it is implicit within the argumentation when the full range of predicates for both the Son and Torah is considered.

So the Son is the superior revelation, both in terms of direct revelation of God as well as the indirect revelation of God understood as the wisdom by which the created order came into being and in which knowledge of God is accessible. The Son who is the wisdom of God embodied is the one who enables embodied human beings to engage Earth in pursuit of the wisdom by which all things are ordered in the quest to know more fully the one who ordered them. Wisdom provides the point of contact through which this identification of human beings and Earth is achieved. What was an aspect of the retrieved voice of Earth in our earlier study becomes the point of identification in this study. "Wisdom christology" once again proves important in teasing out an ecological reading of the christology of Hebrews. So having established a point of identification with Earth in this argumentation, what might Earth have to say to us as a result? To this we now turn in the final section of this discussion.

RETRIEVAL—TO THE ANGELS ONCE AGAIN

The title of this chapter suggests that it is only Heb 2:1–4 that is under investigation. However, as we have seen, this short section is in truth the conclusion to a strand of argumentation that encompasses the entirety of Hebrews to this point. And crucial to the point of 2:1–4 is the comparison of the Son with angels. So in establishing the superiority of the Son over the revelation of Torah, the author had to engage in the comparison involving angels. In the comparison with Torah we found a point of identification between human beings and Earth, forged through a consideration of the claims of the Son and Torah to be the true wisdom of God. At this point, having established this identification via an appeal to wisdom, we might rest content to direct our attention back to ch. 2 where wisdom served in the retrieval of the voice of Earth, and simply state that such is the voice of Earth here as well. This would be a valid conclusion to draw, but there is another aspect of the voice of Earth that comes to the fore from this passage. To find it, however, we must return to the supporting argumentation that gave rise to the author's conclusion in 2:1–4. We must look again at the comparison of the Son with the angels.

In 1:7, Ps 104:4 was cited in the argumentation that established the superior name of the Son over the angels, relegating the angels to the role of serving and worshiping the Son. In reading the author's appropriation of Ps 104:4, one might be tempted to think that a significant focus of the psalm had to do with angels, at least in the Septuagintal version cited by the author, which, as we noted above, modifies the Hebrew text of the psalm to speak of angels as God's servants.[17] This modification makes the LXX version of the passage appealing for the purposes of the author of Hebrews. However, a cursory reading of Ps 104 shows clearly that the focus of the psalm on the whole is a celebration of God's creation in light of God's active involvement in the life of this creation and God's joy in that which God has created.[18]

Brown describes Ps 104 as a "panoramic sweep of creation from the theological and the cosmological to the ecological and the biological, all bracketed by the doxological."[19] The psalm begins with praise for God who is described as majestic and clothed in light (vv. 1–2a). From this opening praise, the psalmist describes in sweeping strokes the initial act of creation (vv. 2b–9). This includes the construction of God's dwelling place in heaven, the foundation of the earth, and the constraining of the chaotic waters.[20] God's role in sustaining this creation is described in vv. 10–23, where God's provision of water for all life (vv. 10–13), food for both human and other than human animal life (vv. 14–15), shelter for all creatures (vv. 16–18), and night and day to order the work of humans and animals in attaining sustenance (vv. 19–23), all highlight God's role in sustaining creation. An interlude (vv. 24–26) follows where the Lord is praised for a creation that manifests the wisdom by which it was made, where the vastness of the sea and its dizzying diversity of life, including the sea monster Leviathan, are cited as examples of God's handiwork.

To this point in Ps 104, we see a picture of God as both creator and sustainer of the universe. Such are the attributes predicated of the Son in

---

17. Ellingworth, *Hebrews*, 120–21, argues that both the Hebrew and LXX versions of the verse essentially make the same point: whether "winds" or "spirit beings" (i.e., "angels"), they are servants of God who are in the argumentation of Hebrews subservient to the Son.

18. Brown, *Seven Pillars of Creation*, 141–59.

19. Ibid., 145.

20. The descriptions in vv. 2b–9 share similarities with the depiction of creation in Job 38–39 and the Egyptian *Hymn to Aten* (*ANET*, 369–71).

Heb 1:2–3a. Disguised from the reader of Heb 1:7 is the rich tapestry of this psalm that celebrates God's creating and sustaining work. And this brings us to one aspect of the voice of Earth suggested by this study: the God who created the angels and subordinated them to the Son also created and actively sustains all of creation, a creation the author of Hebrews tells us was brought into being initially and is sustained continually by the Son. Earth tells us that by reading more deeply than that which is explicitly cited from Ps 104 by the author, we discover a God whose creative and sustaining activities in the world are carried out through the Son who is being extolled as superior to the angels. Indeed, the author of Hebrews has a point to make, but Earth reminds us that there is more to the story in the sources of authority cited by the author than what the author makes plain. And what is more, this creative and sustaining activity of God is extolled as praiseworthy by the psalmist. To borrow from the terminology of the Gen 1 creation account, Ps 104 reminds us that creation remains "good" in the sight of God, and Earth reminds us to keep this observation in mind.

But this is not the entirety of Ps 104. Verses 27–30 introduce a more sobering observation within the created order. The psalmist begins by noting that all creatures are dependent on God for their food, and that when God obliges, they are filled (vv. 27–28). But v. 29 speaks of a God whose face may become hidden, whose breath of life may be withdrawn, with the end results dismay and death. Verse 30 returns to a more positive note, providing a source of hope that indicates that God's breath may yet again bring life and renewal to the world. Yet here is a juxtaposition of death with the strong affirmations of the goodness of life that God has brought into being. This sobering realization sets the stage for the final stanza of the psalm (vv. 31–35). The psalmist begins with an entreaty: "May the glory of the Lord endure forever; may the Lord rejoice in his works" (v. 31). Verse 32 employs imagery of theophany to depict the glory of the Lord in the Earth, to indicate the ongoing presence of God with the world. Following this entreaty, the psalmist again gushes forth in praise, vowing his fidelity and worship to God (v. 34). The final verse of the psalm (v. 35) is a curious conclusion to a psalm that has been so focused on praising God for the creation and sustenance of the world. It includes a prayer for the removal of the sinners from the Earth. It is another aspect of Earth's voice finding expression.

Brown's analysis of Ps 104 sees the psalm as expressing God's passion for and joy in creation as that which is realized in the natural orders God has established and continues to uphold in the world. But, according to Brown, this passion and joy cannot be taken for granted, and so the psalmist goes to great lengths to bring to God's attention creation's vitality and diversity, in an effort to hold God's interest in creation. What can detract from God's joy in creation? The sinners, who might be viewed in the ecological framing of the psalm as those who bring destruction to the beauty of God's world. The destruction of natural habitats contributes to the diminishing of God's joy with creation, and may lead to the hiding of God's face and the removal of God's breath, as described in v. 29.[21] So what is the voice of Earth here? Simply, for human beings to adopt the stance of the psalmist, to break forth in worship and praise for the manifestation of God's wisdom in creation, to remind God continually of the rich beauty and diversity of God's creation, to remind God that it is worthy of divine interest, and to ask God's help in removing from the Earth those things that bring destruction to the natural habitats of the world. In short, Earth may be calling human beings to be doxological intercessors on behalf of Earth.

To summarize, the voice of Earth draws once again on clues seeded in the argumentation of the author of Hebrews to make its pleas to human beings. In this instance, Ps 104, cited by the author for one purpose, is exploited by Earth and mined for its full message. Earth calls us to consider this full message of the psalm, first, to convince us that God indeed finds joy in the creation brought into being by the creative and sustaining agency of the Son, and secondly, to adopt the stance of the psalmist in assuring that God continues to find pleasure in creation as faithful human beings praise God for creation and seek God's guidance in battling the degradation of the ecosystems God has established on the Earth.

CONCLUSION

It is fitting that the final study of this volume returned to the topic with which it began, christology. In truth, all of the studies undertaken here were conversations with the christology of Hebrews. This is, of course, entirely appropriate, given the centrality of christology in the argument of the letter-sermon. In a sense, this study is a continuation of the first study.

---

21. Brown, *Seven Pillars of Creation*, 158–59.

It could have been combined with that first study to make a lengthier, single chapter. However, in the current arrangement, it forms a fitting *inclusio* with the first study for the intervening studies, providing a shape for their understanding.

Perhaps a fitting conclusion for this chapter, and the volume as a whole, is found in the words of St. Athanasius:

> The renewal of creation has been wrought by the Self-same Word Who made it in the beginning. There is thus no inconsistency between creation and salvation; for the One Father has employed the same Agent for both works, effecting the salvation of the world through the same Word Who made it in the beginning.[22]

In the idiom of Hebrews, the same Son who brought the world into being and sustains it also provides for its ultimate redemption. That the argumentation of Hebrews was not concerned with this message has been made abundantly clear. I hope it is equally clear that this message is available when the letter-sermon's argumentation is brought into conversation with an ecological reading of Hebrews.

---

22. Athanasius, *On the Incarnation of the Word of God* 1:4.

9

Conclusion

SO WHERE HAVE WE BEEN?

As is abundantly clear by this point, this study has not been a classical exegetical treatment of the selected texts from Hebrews. It has been a series of readings informed by the ecological hermeneutic developed in the Consultation on Ecological Hermeneutics in the SBL. It has been an ideological reading informed by intertextual and theological readings. So in terms of the structure of this ecological hermeneutic, what have our studies uncovered? Rather than run down a laundry list of findings for each essay, we will attempt a synthesis of our findings.

First, the criterion of *suspicion* was used to discover the biases evident within the pertinent passages. These biases might helpfully be connected to two sets of human interests: the interests of the author and the interests of subsequent interpreters. For the author of Hebrews, there are two overarching interests guiding the rhetoric of the letter-sermon, coupled with a methodological move that helps achieve the aims of the rhetoric. One interest guiding much of the discussion, particularly 1:1—10:16, is a christological interest. In virtually every one of the essays we found that places where issues of ecological importance might have been examined on their own terms, the author of Hebrews, in keeping with the strategic direction of the argumentation, appropriated these issues as data in support of the christological agenda of the letter-sermon. Creative agency, the land, animals, the future destiny of the created order, to name a few, are all mentioned only to support the christological affirmations of the author. Moreover, for our author, along with the christological interest is found a concomitant anthropological interest as well. The benefits of the work of the Son, a substantial component of the author's christological argumentation, are all explicitly assigned to human beings. The other than human creation is not overtly identified as a recipient of the saving work of the Son. So as concerns the author of Hebrews, the criterion of suspicion uncovers a pair of related biases, christological and anthropological in nature.

The methodological move employed by the author is the reinterpretation of facets of the old covenant as they are unfavorably compared to the new covenant instituted by the Son. Frequently such features of the old covenant as the land, the Sabbath rest, the sacrificial cultus, and the promised homeland are spiritualized, or at least relativized, by translating their fulfillment in the Son in terms of heavenly, eternal realities. The net effect is that many entities that might be explored in terms of their ecological significance are reinterpreted or reallocated in terms of the Son and his salvific work on behalf of human beings.

As for subsequent interpreters, at the risk of grossly oversimplifying a rich and diverse engagement with Hebrews through the centuries, we identified two interpretive tendencies, both of which are in keeping with the interests of the author of Hebrews. One such tendency is the thematic appropriation of the argumentation in Hebrews for the subsequent theological reflection of the church. Here attention was frequently directed toward such matters as christological controversies, soteriology (particularly in terms of theories of the atonement), or eschatology. The other interpretive tendency of subsequent interpretation that has affinity with the author of Hebrews is the tendency toward spiritualization. Using Hebrews as an exemplar, interpreters through the ages have found justification for subjecting various components of religious thought to spiritualized reinterpretation. In either case, ecological considerations rarely if ever registered on the radar screens of interpreters of Hebrews.

Second, the criterion of *identification* uncovered areas in which an empathetic connection is evident between the human and other than human parts of creation. Ironically, these points of identification occurred in the same general areas of bias noted above. In the development of the christology of the letter, the author seeded the argumentation with clues that enabled us to forge various points of connection. One such clue is found in the author's treatment of the humanity of the Son. The Son took on human nature in order to secure salvation for human beings (Heb 2:14). But as we saw, there are other scriptural traditions that connect the creation of human beings with Earth via the depiction of human beings as created from the dust of the ground (Gen 2:7). So in becoming human, the Son took upon himself the stuff of Earth in his embodiment. In the person of the Son, human beings and Earth are brought into close connection.

Another aspect of christology that forges an identification between human beings and Earth is the resurrection of the Son. In the argumentation of Hebrews, the bodily resurrection of the Son guarantees the resurrection of those human beings who remain faithful to him. But again, both the Son and human beings share in a very "earthy" embodiment, and this is an embodiment that will undergo glorious transformation in the eschaton. Resurrection, then, identifies human beings and Earth in the final redemption of physicality anticipated by the bodily resurrection of the Son.

One final aspect of christology in our identification between human beings and Earth is the ascension of the Son. The tradition of the Son seated at the right hand of God in an intercessory ministry further demonstrates the connection of human beings with Earth because this resurrected, glorified human being Jesus, by virtue of his current location in heaven, exercises lordship over the Earth. The fact that something of Earth has a place in heaven, and that this glorified human being exercises his lordship through his presence among his people on Earth, anticipates a time when heaven and Earth will be brought together as a dwelling place for God and human beings (Rev 21–22).

The other area of the author's bias that gives rise to an identification between human beings and Earth is anthropology. As noted, human beings derive their creatureliness from the Earth. However, in Gen 2:19, God is said to have created all manner of living creatures out of the dust of the ground. Elsewhere in Genesis, animals are said to possess the "breath of life" (6:7; 7:15, 22) and are designated as "living beings" (2:19), ascriptions given to human beings in 2:7. Moreover, we saw a connection between human beings and Earth in the shared experience of Sabbath rest and in the reliance of human beings on Earth for the elements used in liturgical practices. Creatureliness and religious practice are points of identification between human beings and Earth suggested by the anthropological assertions in Hebrews.

These christological and anthropological reflections evidence how both intertextual and theological readings are brought into the service of the ecological hermeneutic employed here. Their use in teasing out the implications of the author's argumentation suggests that the author was in all likelihood unaware of how the argumentation might suggest an identification between human beings and Earth.

Third, the criterion of *retrieval* brought us to the point of hearing the voice of Earth in light of the previously noted areas of bias and identification. There are three general ways in which we heard the voice of Earth. First, we heard Earth stake a claim as an object of divine care and concern in its own right. The net result of the anthropological bias of the author of Hebrews is that creation might come to be viewed instrumentally as a means toward humanly beneficial ends with little or no regard for how they might affect Earth and its other than human systems of interdependence. Hebrews opens with a statement that the cosmos in its entirety is created through the agency of the Son and that it is sustained by his power. This must include both the human and other than human components of creation. Moreover, the connections of human beings with Earth identified in these studies give credence to the suggestion that at the very least Earth might, in terms of its own integrity as part of God's creative work, fall within the scope of divine care and concern.

The second way in which we heard the voice of Earth closely corresponds to the first. A significant way in which Earth asserts its place in divine care and concern is as a co-beneficiary with human beings of God's redemptive work through the Son. Clearly, the author of Hebrews is concerned with how God has effected human redemption through the superior new covenant of the Son. However, the triad of identification—Son, human beings, Earth—suggests that in his embodiment the Son has accomplished the redemption of all that he was involved in creating and sustaining through his salvific work. The hope entailed in looking toward God's promised eschatological future encompasses both the human and other than human aspects of creation.

The final way in which we heard the voice of Earth derives from the first two. It is a call from Earth for human beings to actualize the realities of new creation in the present in anticipation of eschatological fulfillment. In this manifestation of Earth's voice is the call to action, the call to embody in human life in the world the benefits of the Son's saving work, not just toward other human beings, but also toward all for which God has demonstrated care and concern. We stopped short of developing the specifics of what this might entail. Such an approach will have to wait for a subsequent volume. Here we left the point as a teaser, as an invitation to begin to think creatively and redemptively in the present toward all of God's creation.

One final note. As I presented one of the studies—the one on the recovery of the Eucharist for ecological responsibility—at the SBL annual meeting in Atlanta in 2010, Norm Habel made the observation that my treatment of the retrieval of Earth's voice moved in another direction, that of seeing Earth as a partner in reading the biblical text. Perhaps this approach might prove helpful as we seek a more fully orbed perspective from Earth in and through the biblical text. Seeing Earth as a partner in reading might evidence on our own part as human beings a sense that we are not above Earth functioning as its heroic savior by giving it a voice it otherwise could not have. Rather, we see ourselves in full relationship with Earth, allowing it to shape our reading of the text, hearing its voice not only through our own efforts of unpeeling layers of bias that have kept Earth's voice suppressed, but also on equal terms as fellow interpreters of the text. Perhaps the difference here is more perspectival than substantial. The results of reading may not be radically different whether we read to uncover a suppressed voice or we read in partnership with Earth. The difference perhaps lies in whether we see ourselves as exercising a hermeneutical lordship over Earth or we see ourselves as part of both an ecological and an interpretive community in a relationship of interdependence with Earth.

A FINAL REFLECTION

Schenck has argued that Hebrews draws on story in service of the rhetoric of its argumentation.[1] Despite its homiletical and epistolary modes of presentation, Hebrews is connected with aspects of the biblical drama that necessarily involve it in the larger story of God's redemption of human beings. Schenck's reading of the text in light of this story leads him to the conclusion that the physical world, the other than human creation, is simply the stage on which the drama of human redemption in the Son takes place, and that it is destined for destruction following the fulfillment of its role in the story. His reading of Hebrews brings out those aspects of the letter-sermon that fuel some strands of popular eschatological fervor that have as a side effect the diminution of Earth.

---

1. K. Schenck, *Understanding the Book of Hebrews*.

I find much to commend Schenck's approach to reading Hebrews, particularly in his understanding of how Hebrews reflects the underlying narrative logic of the biblical drama of redemption. My critique of Schenck at this point is not his connection of Hebrews to the biblical drama, but his limitation of the scope of that drama to human redemption, at least at the level of its appropriation by the author of Hebrews. The approach of our study has been to employ an ecological hermeneutic that is anchored to the biblical drama of salvation, but one that self-consciously draws from a wider depiction of redemptive narrative.

In the final analysis, the ecological hermeneutic employed in this study makes no claims to be the "right" or "true" or even "best" way to read the biblical texts. It is not an approach that denies more traditional readings and approaches to the study of Hebrews. Rather, it is an approach that pursues particular entry points into the text for the purpose of examining one set of concerns. In the final analysis, it is a way of reading that takes one point of view, that of Earth, in order to facilitate a conversation, one not just about the interpretation of Hebrews, but also one of much larger scope, the conduct of faithful human living on planet Earth.

Bibliography

Adams, Edward. "The Cosmology of Hebrews." In *The Epistle to the Hebrews and Christian Theology*, edited by Richard Bauckham et al., 122–39. Grand Rapids: Eerdmans, 2009.

Allen, David M. "'The Forgotten Spirit': A Pentecostal Reading of the Letter to the Hebrews." *Journal of Pentecostal Theology* 18 (2009) 51–66.

Andriessen, Paul. "L'Eucharist dans l'Épître aux Hébreux." *Nouvelle Revue Théologique* 94 (1972) 269–77.

Athanasius. *On the Incarnation of the Word of God*. New York: Macmillan, 1946.

Attridge, Harold W. *The Epistle to the Hebrews*. Hermeneia. Philadelphia: Fortress, 1989.

Balabanski, Vicky. "Critiquing Anthropocentric Cosmology: Retrieving a Stoic 'Permeation Cosmology' in Colossians 1:15–20." In *Exploring Ecological Hermeneutics*, edited by Norman C. Habel and Peter Trudinger, 151–59. Symposium Series 46. Atlanta: SBL, 2008.

———. "John 1—the Earth Bible Challenge: An Intra-textual Approach to Reading John 1." In *The Earth Story in the New Testament*, edited by Norman C. Habel and Vicky Balabanski, 89–94. Earth Bible 5. London: Sheffield Academic, 2002.

Bauckham, Richard, et al. *A Cloud of Witnesses: The Theology of Hebrews in Its Ancient Contexts*. London: T. & T. Clark, 2008.

———. *The Epistle to the Hebrews and Christian Theology*. Grand Rapids: Eerdmans, 2009.

Bauer, Walter, Frederick W. Danker, W. F. Arndt, and F. W. Gingrich. *Greek-English Lexicon of the New Testament and Other Early Christian Literature*. 3rd ed. Chicago: University of Chicago Press, 2000.

Beale, Gregory K. *The Temple and the Church's Mission: A Biblical Theology of the Dwelling Place of God*. Downers Grove, IL: IVP, 2004.

Beck, T. David. *The Holy Spirit and the Renewal of All Things: Pneumatology in Paul and Jürgen Moltmann*. Eugene, OR: Pickwick, 2007.

Beekman, John, and John Callow. *Translating the Word of God*. Grand Rapids: Zondervan, 1974.

Bergant, Dianne. "The Wisdom of Solomon." In *Readings from the Perspective of Earth*, edited by Norman C. Habel, 138–50. Earth Bible 1. Sheffield: Sheffield Academic, 2000.

Boff, Leonardo. *Cry of the Earth, Cry of the Poor*. Maryknoll, NY: Orbis, 1997.

Brown, William P. *The Seven Pillars of Creation: The Bible, Science, and the Ecology of Wisdom*. Oxford: Oxford University Press, 2010.

Bruce, F. F. *The Epistle to the Hebrews*. New International Commentary on the New Testament. Rev. ed. Grand Rapids: Eerdmans, 1990.

Buchanan, George W. *To the Hebrews*. Anchor Bible. Garden City, NY: Doubleday, 1972.

Cain, Clifford C. *An Ecological Theology: Reunderstanding Our Relation to Nature*. Lewiston, NY: Edwin Mellen, 2009.

Bibliography

Carlay, Keith. "Psalm 8: An Apology for Domination." In *Readings from the Perspective of Earth*, edited by Norman C. Habel, 111–24. Earth Bible 1. Sheffield: Sheffield Academic, 2000.

Cadwallader, Alan H. "Earth as Host or Stranger?: Reading Hebrews 11 from Diasporan Experience." In *The Earth Story in the New Testament*, edited by Norman C. Habel and Vicky Balabanski, 148–65. Earth Bible 5. London: Sheffield Academic, 2002.

Charlesworth, James H., editor. *The Old Testament Pseudepigrapha*. 2 vols. New York: Doubleday, 1983–1985.

Clifford, Richard J. "The Hebrew Scriptures and the Theology of Creation." *Theological Studies* 46 (1985) 507–23.

Clifton, Shane. "Preaching the 'Full Gospel' in the Context of Global Environmental Crises." In *The Spirit Renews the Face of the Earth: Pentecostal Forays in Science and Theology of Creation*, edited by Amos Yong, 117–34. Eugene, OR: Pickwick, 2009.

Cooperman, Alan. "Evangelical Angers Peers With Call for Action on Global Warming." *Washington Post* (3 March 2007) A04.

Craddock, Fred B. *Hebrews*. New Interpreter's Bible. Nashville: Abingdon, 1998.

Danby, Herbert, editor. *The Mishnah*. New York: Oxford University Press, 1933.

Davidson, Ivor J. "Pondering the Sinlessness of Jesus Christ: Moral Christologies and the Witness of Scripture." *International Journal of Systematic Theology* 10 (2008) 372–98.

Edwards, Denis. *Ecology at the Heart of Faith*. Maryknoll, NY: Orbis, 2006.

Ellingworth, Paul. *The Epistle to the Hebrews*. New International Greek Testament Commentary. Grand Rapids: Eerdmans, 1991.

Emmrich, Martin. "Hebrews 6:4–6—Again! (A Pneumatological Inquiry)." *Westminster Theological Journal* 65 (2003) 83–95.

Euripides. *The Madness of Hercules*. Translated by Arthur Sanders Way. Loeb Classical Library. Cambridge: Harvard University Press, 1971.

Fee, Gordon. *Pauline Christology*. Peabody, MA: Hendrickson, 2007.

Fretheim, Terence. *The Book of Genesis*. New Interpreter's Bible. Nashville: Abingdon, 1994.

Gaiser, Frederick, and Mark Throntveit, editors. *"And God Saw That It Was Good." Essays on Creation and God in Honor of Terence Freitheim*. Word and World Supplement Series 5. St. Paul: Word and World, Luther Seminary, 2006.

Gammie, John G., editor. *Israelite Wisdom: Theological and Literary Essays in Honor of Samuel Terrien*. Missoula, MT: Scholars, 1978.

Gaston, Lloyd. *Paul and the Torah*. Vancouver: University of British Columbia Press, 1987.

Green Bible, The. New York: HarperOne, 2008.

Green, Joel B., editor. *What About the Soul? Neuroscience and Christian Anthropology*. Nashville: Abingdon, 2004.

Grey, Jacqueline. "'The Trees of the Field Will Clap Their Hands': Is There Hope for the Renewal of Creation in Second Isaiah?" Paper presented at the annual meeting of the Society for Pentecostal Studies, Eugene, OR, 27 March 2009.

Habel, Norman C., editor. *The Earth Story in Psalms and Prophets*. Earth Bible 4. Sheffield: Sheffield Academic, 2001.

———. "An Ecojustice Challenge: Is Earth Valued in John 1?" In *The Earth Story in the New Testament*, edited by Norman C. Habel and Vicky Balabanski, 76–82. Earth Bible 5. London: Sheffield Academic, 2002.

———. *An Inconvenient Text: Is a Green Reading of the Bible Possible?* Hindmarsh, Australia: ATF, 2009.

———. "Introducing Ecological Hermeneutics." In *Exploring Ecological Hermeneutics*, edited by Norman C. Habel and Peter Trudinger, 1–8. Symposium Series 46. Atlanta: SBL, 2008.
———. *The Land Is Mine: Six Biblical Images*. Minneapolis: Fortress, 1995.
———. "The Origins and Challenges of an Ecojustice Hermeneutic." In *Relating to the Text: Interdisciplinary and Form-Critical Insights on the Bible*, edited by Timothy J. Sandoval and Carleen Mandolfo, 141–59. London: T. & T. Clark, 2003.
———. "Playing God or Playing Earth? An Ecological Reading of Genesis 1.26–28." In *"And God Saw That It Was Good." Essays on Creation and God in Honor of Terence Freitheim*, edited by Frederick Gaiser and Mark Throntveit, 33–41. Word and World Supplement Series 5. St. Paul: Word and World, Luther Seminary, 2006.
———, editor. *Readings from the Perspective of Earth*. Earth Bible 1. Sheffield: Sheffield Academic, 2000.
Habel, Norman C., and Vicky Balabanski, editors. *The Earth Story in the New Testament*. Earth Bible 5. Sheffield: Sheffield Academic, 2002.
Habel, Norman C., and Peter Trudinger, editors. *Exploring Ecological Hermeneutics*. Symposium Series 46. Atlanta: SBL, 2008.
Habel, Norman C., and Shirley Wurst, editors. *The Earth Story in Genesis*. Earth Bible 2. Sheffield: Sheffield Academic, 2000.
———. *The Earth Story in Wisdom Traditions*. Earth Bible 3. Sheffield: Sheffield Academic, 2001.
Hahne, Harry A. *The Corruption and Redemption of Creation: Nature in Romans 8:19–22 and Jewish Apocalyptic Literature*. Library of New Testament Studies 336. London: T. & T. Clark, 2006.
Harris, Murray J. *Jesus as God: The New Testament Use of* Theos *in Reference to Jesus*. Grand Rapids: Baker, 1992.
Heen, Erik M., and Philip D. W. Krey, editors. *Hebrews*. Ancient Christian Commentary on Scripture. Downers Grove, IL: IVP Academic, 2005.
Hillel, Daniel. *The Natural History of the Bible: An Environmental Exploration of the Hebrew Scriptures*. New York: Columbia University Press, 2006.
Hobgood-Oster, Laura. *The Friends We Keep: Unleashing Christianity's Compassion for Animals*. Waco: Baylor University Press, 2010.
Hogue, Michael S. *The Tangled Bank: Toward an Ecotheological Ethics of Responsible Participation*. Eugene, OR: Pickwick, 2008.
Holmes, Michael W., editor. *The Apostolic Fathers in English*. 3rd ed. Grand Rapids: Baker Academic, 2006.
Huff, Peter A. "Calvin and the Beasts: Animals in John Calvin's Theological Discourse." *Journal of the Evangelical Theological Society* 42 (March 1999) 67–75.
Jewett, Robert. *Letter to Pilgrims: A Commentary on the Epistle to the Hebrews*. New York: Pilgrim Press, 1981.
Johnson, Luke Timothy. *Hebrews*. New Testament Library. Louisville: Westminster John Knox, 2006.
Josephus. *Jewish Antiquities, Books 14–15*. Translated by Ralph Marcus and Allen Wikgren. Loeb Classical Library. Cambridge: Harvard University Press, 1943.
Koester, Craig R. *Hebrews*. Anchor Bible. New York: Doubleday, 2001.
Kolarcik, Michael. *The Book of Wisdom*. New Interpreter's Bible. Nashville: Abingdon, 1997.

Laansma, Jon. "Hidden Stories in Hebrews: Cosmology and Theology." In *A Cloud of Witnesses: The Theology of Hebrews in Its Ancient Contexts*, edited by Richard Bauckham et al., 9–18. London: T. & T. Clark, 2008.
Lamp, Jeffrey S. *First Corinthians 1–4 in Light of Jewish Wisdom Traditions: Christ, Wisdom, and Spirituality*. Lampeter: Edwin Mellen, 2000.
Lane, William L. *Hebrews 1–8*. Word Biblical Commentary. Dallas: Word, 1991.
———. *Hebrews 9–13*. Word Biblical Commentary. Dallas: Word, 1991.
Lella, Alexander A. di. "Conservative and Progressive Theology: Sirach and Wisdom." *Catholic Biblical Quarterly* 28 (1966) 139–54.
Levinson, Jon D. "Observations on the Creation Theology in Wisdom." In *Israelite Wisdom: Theological and Literary Essays in Honor of Samuel Terrien*, edited by John G. Gammie, 43–57. Missoula, MT: Scholars, 1978.
Linzey, Andrew. *Animal Gospel: Christian Faith as if Animals Mattered*. Louisville: Westminster John Knox, 2000.
———. "C. S. Lewis' Theology of Animals." *Anglican Theological Review* 80 (Winter 1998) 60–81.
Lodahl, Michael. *God of Nature and of Grace: Reading the World in a Wesleyan Way*. Nashville: Kingswood, 2003.
Luz, Ulrich. *Matthew in History: Interpretation, Influence, and Effects*. Minneapolis: Fortress, 1994.
Macchia, Frank. *Baptized in the Spirit: A Global Pentecostal Theology*. Grand Rapids: Zondervan, 2006.
McGrath, John J. *"Through the Eternal Spirit": An Historical Study of the Exegesis of Hebrews 9:13–14*. Rome: Pontificia Universitas Gregoriana, 1961.
Moltmann, Jürgen. *God in Creation: A New Theology of Creation and the Spirit of God*. Translated by Margaret Kohl. Minneapolis: Fortress, 1993.
———. *The Spirit of Life: A Universal Affirmation*. Translated by Margaret Kohl. Minneapolis: Fortress, 2001.
Murphy, Roland. *The Tree of Life*. 3rd ed. Grand Rapids: Eerdmans, 2002.
Neal, Ryan A. *Theology as Hope: On the Ground and Implications of Jürgen Moltmann's Doctrine of Hope*. Eugene, OR: Pickwick, 2008.
Neusner, Jacob, editor. *The Babylonian Talmud: A New Translation and Commentary*. 22 vols. Rev. ed. Peabody, MA: Hendrickson, 2011.
Northcott, Michael S. *The Environment and Christian Ethics*. New Studies in Christian Ethics. Cambridge: Cambridge University Press, 1996.
O'Brien, Peter T. *The Letter to the Hebrews*. Pillar New Testament Commentary. Grand Rapids: Eerdmans, 2010.
Philo. Translated by F. H. Colson et al. Loeb Classical Library. Cambridge: Harvard University Press, 1929–1962.
Philostratus. *The Life of Apollonius of Tyana, Volume 1*. Translated and edited by Christopher P. Jones. Loeb Classical Library. Cambridge: Harvard University Press, 2005.
Pinnock, Clark. *Flame of Love*. Downers Grove, IL: InterVarsity Press, 1996.
Plato. *Timaeus*. Translated by R. G. Bury. Loeb Classical Library. Cambridge: Harvard University Press, 1929.
Pritchard, James B., editor. *Ancient Near Eastern Texts Relating to the Old Testament*. 3rd ed. Princeton: Princeton University Press, 1969.
Rad, Gerhard von. *Genesis: A Commentary*. Rev. ed. London: SCM, 1972.

Richter, Sandra L. "Environmental Law in Deuteronomy: One Lens on a Biblical Theology for Creation Care." *Bulletin for Biblical Research* 20 (2010) 355–76.
Schenck, Kenneth L. *Cosmology and Eschatology in Hebrews: The Settings of the Sacrifice.* Cambridge: Cambridge University Press, 2007.
———. "God Has Spoken: Hebrews' Theology of the Scriptures." In *The Epistle to the Hebrews and Christian Theology*, edited by Richard Bauckham et al., 321–36. Grand Rapids: Eerdmans, 2009.
———. *Understanding the Book of Hebrews: The Story Behind the Sermon.* Louisville: Westminster John Knox, 2005.
Seneca. *Moral Essays, Volume 3. De Beneficiis.* Translated by John W. Basor. Loeb Classical Library. Cambridge: Harvard University Press, 1935.
Shemesh, Yael. "'And Many Beasts' (Jonah 4:11): The Function and Status of Animals in the Book of Jonah." *Journal of Hebrew Scriptures* 10 (2010). No pages. Online: http://www.arts.ualberta.ca/JHS/Articles/article_134.pdf.
Singer, Peter. *Animal Liberation.* Rev. ed. London: Pimlico, 1995.
Solivan, Samuel. *The Spirit, Pathos, and Liberation: Towards a Hispanic Pentecostal Theology.* Sheffield: Sheffield Academic, 1998.
Stone, Lawson G. "The Soul: Possession, Part, or Person? The Genesis of Human Nature in Genesis 2:7." In *What About the Soul? Neuroscience and Christian Anthropology*, edited by Joel B. Green, 47–61. Nashville: Abingdon, 2004.
Swetnam, James. "Christology and the Eucharist in the Epistle to the Hebrews." *Biblica* 70 (1989) 74–95.
Tallman, Matthew. "Pentecostal Ecology: A Theological Paradigm." In *The Spirit Renews the Face of the Earth: Pentecostal Forays in Science and Theology of Creation*, edited by Amos Yong, 135–54. Eugene, OR: Pickwick, 2009.
Thurén, J. *Das Lobopfer der Hebräer: Studien zum Aufbau und Anliegen von Hebräerbrief 13.* Åbo: Åbo Akademi, 1973.
Treier, Daniel. "Speech Acts, Hearing Hearts, and Other Senses: The Doctrine of Scripture Practiced in Hebrews." In *The Epistle to the Hebrews and Christian Theology*, edited by Richard Bauckham et al., 337–50. Grand Rapids: Eerdmans, 2009.
Turner, Marie. "The Spirit of Wisdom in All Things: The Mutuality of Earth and Humankind." In *Exploring Ecological Hermeneutics*, edited by Norman C. Habel and Peter Trudinger, 113–22. Symposium Series 46. Atlanta: Society of Biblical Literature, 2008.
Wade, Richard. "Towards a Christian Ethics of Animals." *Pacifica* 13 (June 2000) 202–12.
Wainwright, Elaine. "Which Intertext? A Response to 'An Ecojustice Challenge: Is Earth Valued in John 1?'" In *The Earth Story in the New Testament*, edited by Norman C. Habel and Vicky Balabanski, 83–88. Earth Bible 5. London: Sheffield Academic, 2002.
Walton, John H. *Ancient Near Eastern Thought and the Old Testament: Introducing the Conceptual World of the Hebrew Bible.* Grand Rapids: Baker, 2006.
Williamson, R. "The Eucharist and the Epistle to the Hebrews." *New Testament Studies* 21 (1975) 300–312.
Winston, David. *The Wisdom of Solomon.* Anchor Bible. New York: Doubleday, 1979.
Wise, Michael O., et al. *The Dead Sea Scrolls: A New Translation.* Rev. ed. New York: HarperCollins, 2005.
Witherington, Ben, III. *Letters and Homilies for Jewish Christians.* Downers Grove, IL: IVP Academic, 2007.

Wright, N. T. *The Resurrection of the Son of God*. Minneapolis: Fortress, 2003.
———. *Surprised by Hope*. New York: HarperOne, 2008.
Yong, Amos, editor. *The Spirit Renews the Face of the Earth: Pentecostal Forays in Science and Theology of Creation*. Eugene, OR: Pickwick, 2009.
Zizioulas, John. "Preserving God's Creation: Three Lectures on Ecology and Theology." *King's Theological Review* 12 (1989) 1–5, 41–45; and 13 (1990) 1–5.

Author Index

Adams, Edward, 81n28
Allen, David M., 52n1
Andriessen, Paul, 88n4
Attridge, Harold W., 15n8, 30n17, 39n2, 52n3, 54n12, 55n15, 55n19, 56n21, 59n31, 72n8, 75n15, 88n5, 102n1, 105n10

Balabanski, Vicky, 4n6, 20n17
Beale, Gregory K., 49n27
Beck, T. David, 56n22, 63n38
Beekman, John, 104n5
Bergant, Dianne, 16n9
Boff, Leonardo, 66, 66n49
Brown, William P., 46n18, 109–11, 109nn18–19, 111n21
Bruce, F. F., 15n8, 31n19, 39n2, 42n9, 52n3, 54nn10–11, 55, 55n14, 55n18, 60n33, 81, 81n29, 88n5, 89nn8–9, 94n15, 105n12
Buchanan, George W., 16n11, 27n13, 40–41, 41nn6–7, 52n3, 53n5, 54n10, 54n12, 76, 76n18, 87n1

Cain, Clifford C., 49n29
Callow, John, 104n5
Carlay, Keith, 12n4
Cadwallader, Alan H., 41n7, 69–70, 70n1, 82, 82n34
Clifford, Richard J., 14n7
Clifton, Shane, 66, 67n51
Cooperman, Alan, 12n2
Craddock, Fred B., 13n5, 15n8, 26n10, 40n3, 42n10, 47n23,
54n10, 54n12, 55n15, 55n18, 56n20, 73n9, 73n11, 74n12, 76n19, 87n1, 88n5, 90n12, 94n15

Davidson, Ivor J., 61n36

Edwards, Denis, 90n13, 91–92, 91n14, 97–98, 97n18
Ellingworth, Paul, 39n2, 41n7, 52n2, 53n7, 54n12, 55n14, 55n18, 56n21, 75n15, 88n5, 100n20, 103–4n5, 109n17
Emmrich, Martin, 54n13

Fee, Gordon, 16n10
Freitheim, Terence, 23n2

Gaston, Lloyd, 106n15
Grey, Jacqueline, 46n18

Habel, Norman C., 4, 4nn4–6, 5nn7–8, 9n10, 12, 12n3, 20n17, 23n3, 43, 43nn12–13, 45, 45n16, 82, 82n32, 117
Hahne, Harry A., 83–84, 83n35
Harris, Murray J., 104, 104n8
Hillel, Daniel, 43n12
Hobgood-Oster, Laura, 35n34
Hogue, Michael S., 33n25, 34, 34nn30–31
Huff, Peter A., 33n27

Jewett, Robert, 10–11n1, 40n3, 46–47, 47nn19–20, 82, 82n33

Johnson, Luke Timothy, 15n8, 18n16, 25, 25n7, 26nn10–11, 27n12, 29n14, 29n16, 30n18, 39n2, 42n8, 42n11, 47nn22–23, 52n2, 53n6, 55n16, 56nn20–21, 75n15, 88n5, 100n20

Koester, Craig R., 15n8, 18n16, 25n8, 29n16, 39n2, 47n21, 52n3, 53n7, 55n14, 56n21, 60n34, 71n4, 73n10, 74n12, 75n13, 81, 81n30, 88n5, 100n20

Kolarcik, Michael, 16n8, 17n13

Laansma, Jon, 48–49n27, 80, 80n25
Lamp, Jeffrey S., 106n14, 107n16
Lane, William L., 15–16n8, 29n15, 40nn3–4, 42n8, 48n25, 52n2, 53n5, 53n7, 54n10, 54n12, 55n18, 56n21, 59n29, 60n33, 73n11, 75n14, 76n19, 79–80, 80nn23–24, 81–82n31, 88nn5–6, 102–3n2, 103n4, 104n6, 104n9, 105n10
Lella, Alexander A. di, 17n14
Levinson, Jon D., 14n7
Linzey, Andrew, 33n26, 35–36, 36n35
Lodahl, Michael, 33n28
Luz, Ulrich, 95–96, 96n17, 100n20

Macchia, Frank, 65–66, 65nn45–46, 66nn47–48
McGrath, John J., 55n17, 59–60, 59n30, 59n32, 60n35
Moltmann, Jürgen, 48n26, 51, 56–58, 56n22, 57nn23–26, 58n28, 61n36, 62–65, 63n37, 63n39, 64nn40–43, 67
Murphy, Roland, 14n7

Neal, Ryan A., 56n22

Northcott, Michael S., 30n17, 40n5, 45n17, 48n26

O'Brien, Peter T., 16n10, 26n11, 39n2, 52n2, 55n15, 55n18, 80n23, 88, 88nn5–7, 94n15, 102n1, 103n5, 104nn5–7, 104n9, 105n10, 105n12

Pinnock, Clark, 66, 66n50

Rad, Gerhard von, 23n2
Richter, Sandra, 44n14, 48n24, 49n28

Schenck, Kenneth L., 3n3, 10n1, 40n3, 53n4, 71n3, 72nn6–7, 75–76, 75n16, 76n17, 117–18, 117n1
Shemesh, Yael, 31n21
Singer, Peter, 34, 34n33
Solivan, Samuel, 65n44
Stone, Lawson G., 33n25
Swetnam, James, 87n2

Tallman, Matthew, 67n51
Thurén, J., 87n2
Trier, Daniel, 53n4
Turner, Marie, 16n9

Wade, Richard, 23n4, 34, 34nn32–33
Wainwright, Elaine, 20n17
Walton, John H., 49n27
Williamson, R., 87–88, 87n2, 88n3, 89, 89nn10–11
Winston, David, 16n8
Witherington, Ben, III, 30n17, 40n3, 53n7, 54n12, 55n18, 80–81, 80nn26–27, 88n5
Wright, N. T., 70n2, 77–79, 84
Wurst, Shirley 4n6

Zizioulas, John, 90n13, 91

Ancient Document Index

ANCIENT NEAR EASTERN DOCUMENTS

Hymn to Aten — 109n20

OLD TESTAMENT/ HEBREW BIBLE

Genesis

Reference	Page
1	110
1:20–25	23
1:21	23
1:25	23
1:26–28	12–13
1:26–27	23
1:26	49
2	32, 49
2:2–3	37
2:2	40n4, 42, 42n9, 47–49
2:3	48
2:7	13, 23, 31–32, 61, 77, 114–15
2:15	49
2:18–19	23
2:19	31–32, 115
2:20	23
3	49
3:21	23
4:4	23
6:7	23, 115
6:17	32
7:2–3	23
7:15	32, 115
7:22	32, 115
9:2–3	24
9:8–16	23–24
12:1	73
14:17	93
14:18–20	92–93
15:7–21	24
15:9–21	29n15
22	76
22:13	24
24:37	82

Exodus

Reference	Page
19	103
20	103
23:4–5	24
23:10–12	43
23:11	24
23:12	24
24:3–8	29n15
29:12	29n15

Leviticus

Reference	Page
4:17	29n15
4:18	29n15
4:25	29n15
4:30	29n15
4:34	29n15
7:6	87
8:15	29n15
9:9	29n15
17:11	30n17
18:24–28	44n15
25—27	43
25:10	43–44

Leviticus (cont.)

25:18–22	44
25:23	43
26:3–45	44–46
26:3–13	44
26:14–45	44–46
26:33	45
26:34–35	44–45
26:40–45	45–46
26:42	45

Numbers

14	40
18:9–10	87

Deuteronomy

5:14	24
25:4	24
28:1–24	44n15
29:22–29	44n15
32:43	104
33:2	103

1 Samuel

7:14	103
15:22	26

Job

33:4	63–64
34:13–14	63–64
38–39	109n20

Psalms

2:7	103
8	12
8:1	12
8:3	12–13
8:4–6	12–13
8:5–7 LXX	12
8:9	12
39	26–27, 28
39:6–8 LXX	26, 61
44:7–8 LXX	104
45:6–7	104
50:5	29n15
94:7–11 LXX	42
95	40, 49n27, 53
95:7–11	42
95:7	42
95:9 LXX	80
95:11	42, 42n11, 47
96:7 LXX	104
96:9	80
97:7	104
101:26–28 LXX	72, 104
102:25–27	104–5
102:26–28	72
103:4 LXX	104
104	109–11
104:1–2a	109
104:2b–9	109
104:4	104–5, 109
104:10–23	109
104:10–13	109
104:14–15	109
104:16-18	109
104:19–23	109
104:24–26	109
104:27–30	110
104:27–28	110
104:29–30	63–64
104:29	110–11
104:30	110
104:31–35	110
104:31	110
104:32	110
104:34	110
104:35	110
110	93
110:1	104
110:4	92–93
139:7–9	66–67
150:6	31

Proverbs

1:20	18
3:19–20	14
8:22–31	14

Ecclesiastes

3:19	32n23

Isaiah

1:10–13	26
7:23–25	45
8:21–22	45
9:18–21	45
13:1–22	79–80
24:4–6	45
32:9–14	45
33:7–9	45
34:8–17	45
41:8–20	45
42:1–13	45
42:1	60
44:24	46n18
45:12	46n18
48:13	46n18
49:1–13	45
50:4—51:3	45
51:13	46n18
52:13—55:13	45–46
54:1–3	46n18
61:1	60
65:25	31

Jeremiah

4:23–26	45
7:21–24	26
31:31–34	24, 53, 54n9
31:33–34	24
34:17–20	29n15
38:31–34 LXX	24
38:33–34 LXX	24

Hosea

6:6	26

Amos

4:7–9	45
5:21–26	26

Micah

6:6–8	26

Haggai

2:6	75, 79–80

APOCRYPHA

Wisdom of Solomon

7:17	16
7:18–20	16
7:22—8:1	14–17, 106–7
7:22	16
7:23	16
7:26	16
7:27	16
7:28	16
8:1	16

Sirach

24:23	106
33:3	106
39:1	106

Baruch

3:15—4:1	106

4 Maccabees

1:16–17	106

PSEUDEPIGRAPHA

1 Enoch

45:1	79–80

2 Baruch

4:1–4	73
32:1	79–80
59:3	79–80
73:6	31n22

2 Enoch

51:5	31n20
55:2	73
58:5	31n22

4 Ezra

5:48	32n24
7:26	73
7:62	32n24
7:116	32n24
8:52	73
10:27	73

Apocalypse of Moses

11:2–3	23n5

Jubilees

1:27	103
1:29	79–80
2:1	103
2:26–27	103
5:2	23n5
5:4	23n5
5:12	23n6
5:20	23n5

Sib. Or.

3:675–80	79–80

~

NEW TESTAMENT

Matthew

6:10	78
12:28	65

Luke

12:24	24

John

1:10	10, 13n6
1:14	13n6

Acts

7:38	103
7:53	103
28:25	53

Romans

1:4	57, 62, 65
6	78
8:2	60n35
8:11	62
8:18–27	62
8:18–25	19
8:19–27	65
8:19–21	31, 64
8:19–22	83
8:19-23	24
8:21	19

1 Corinthians

8:6	10, 16n10
9:9–10	24
12:11	52
15:45	57

2 Corinthians

3:2–3	107

Galatians

3:19	103

Ephesians

2:21–22	40

Colossians

1:15–20	92
1:16–17	10, 16n10
1:16	64
1:20	64
1:26	11n1

Hebrews

1:1—10:16	113
1:1—4:13	48n27

Hebrews (*cont.*)

1:1—2:4	103
1	12
1:1–4	101
1:1–3	102–3, 103n2
1:1–2	18n16
1:1	53, 102, 102n2
1:2–3	102, 104
1:2–3a	2, 10–20, 28, 31, 77, 92, 101–2, 106–7, 109–10
1:2	16–17, 64, 102–3
1:3	16, 16n11, 47, 64, 77
1:4–14	72
1:4	102, 102–3n2
1:5–14	102–6, 104n8
1:5–13	103
1:5	103–5
1:6	103–4
1:7–12	104
1:7	104–5, 105n11, 109–10
1:8–9	104
1:8	104
1:8a	72
1:10–12	69, 72, 104–5
1:10	104
1:12	104
1:13	77, 104–5
1:14	105
2	12
2:1–4	101–12
2:2–3	103
2:2	102
2:3	52, 53, 103
2:4	51, 52–53, 54
2:5	81
2:6–7	12
2:9	77n20
2:10	10n1, 39, 105
2:14–18	60
2:14–15	19
2:14	13, 31, 61, 77, 114
3:4	10n1
3:7—4:13	49n27
3:7–19	42

3:7	40, 51, 53–54, 55
3:11	42
3:13	40, 53
3:15	40, 53
4	42–43
4:1–11	37–50, 53, 69, 71–72
4:2	48
4:3	10n1, 40
4:4	37, 40n4, 42
4:6	40
4:7	40, 53
4:8	38
4:9	40, 42
4:10	39–40, 48
4:11	39
4:14—10:25	48–49n27
4:14	88
4:15	60, 88
4:16	60
5:1	26n9
5:3	26n9
5:6	60, 93
5:7–8	60
5:10	93
5:11–14	54
6:1–5	100n20
6:1–3	54
6:2	76, 100n20
6:4–6	54–55
6:4–5	54
6:4	51
6:19	88
6:20	60, 93
7	24–25, 93–95
7:1–10	93–94
7:1–2a	93–94
7:3	94
7:4	94
7:11	93
7:15–22	60
7:15	93
7:16	60n35
7:17	93

Hebrews (cont.)

7:25	47, 77
7:27	26n9
8:1	24, 77, 88
8:8–12	24
8:8	54n9
9:1–10	25
9:1	61
9:6–7	59
9:7	26n9
9:8–9	72n7
9:8	51, 55
9:9	25, 26n9, 60, 76n19
9:10	25, 100n20
9:11—10:18	21–36
9:12	26, 60n34
9:13	25–26, 59
9:14	51–68
9:15–18	29n15
9:15	26
9:19	25–26, 30n17
9:22	29n15
9:25	26n9, 59
9:28	59–60
10	61
10:1–4	59
10:1	26n9
10:2–3	30n18
10:3	26n9
10:4–5	61
10:4	26
10:5–10	26, 29n14
10:6	28
10:8–9	26n9
10:10	26, 59–60
10:11	26n9
10:12	59, 77
10:14	26, 60
10:15	51, 53–54, 53n9, 55
10:16–17	24
10:19–25	71
10:19–22	60
10:19	88
10:29	51, 56
11	41n7, 82
11:1	72
11:3	10n1
11:8–16	39, 69–85
11:8	72–73
11:9	72–73
11:10	73, 80–81, 89
11:13	72–73, 82
11:15	74
11:17–19	76
11:19	76–77
11:35	76–77
12:2	77
12:15–17	74
12:18–29	72, 74–75, 79–80
12:18–21	74
12:18	74
12:21	74
12:22–28	69
12:22–27	39
12:22–24	71–72, 74–75
12:22	73
12:25–29	75, 80
12:26	75
12:27	75
12:28	75
13:9–16	96
13:9	88
13:10–16	87
13:10	85–100
13:11	26n9, 87, 87n1
13:12	85–88
13:13	87
13:14	81
13:15–16	30, 87
13:15	86
13:16	86
13:20–25	2n2
13:20	77

1 Peter

2:5	40

Revelation

3:14	10
21—22	64, 78, 115
21:2	73, 81
21:10	73, 81

DEAD SEA SCROLLS

1QS

9:4–5	31n19

4QFlor

1:6	31n19

1QH

1:28	31n19

CD

5:18	103

Philo

Creation

3	106

Fug.

112	17n12

Leg.

3:83	73

Migr.

6	17n12
89–93	31n19

Plant.

8	17n12
50	18n15
126–35	31n19

Somn.

2:250	73

Spec. Laws

1:81	17n15
1:267–72	31n19

Josephus

Ant.

15:5:3	103
15:36	103

RABBINIC WRITINGS

b. Menaḥ.

93b	29n15

b. Yoma

5a	29n15

b. Zebaḥ.

6a	29n15

m. Soṭah

9:6	53

Pirqe Abot

3:23	106

GRECO-ROMAN WRITINGS

Euripides

Madness of Hercules

1345	31n19

Philostratus

Life of Apollonius

1:1	31n19

Plato

Timaeus

92C	17n15

Seneca

De beneficiis

1:6:3   31n19

EARLY CHRISTIAN WRITINGS

1 Clem.

13:1   53
16:2   53

Athanasius

On the Incarnation of the Word

1:4   112

Clement of Alexandria

Stromateis

4:25   94n16

Cyprian

Letter

62:4   94n16

Diognetus

3:3–5   31n19
5:5–9   81n31
5:9   81n31

Epiphanus of Salamis

Against Melchizedekians

6:1–11   94n16

Panarion

4   94n16

Eusebius of Caesarea

Proof of the Gospel

5:3   94n16

Gregory of Nyssa

On the Lord's Prayer

3   65–66, 66n47

Jerome

Hebrew Questions on Genesis

14:18–19   94n16

Shepherd of Hermas

Similitude

1:1   82n31

www.ingramcontent.com/pod-product-compliance
Lightning Source LLC
Chambersburg PA
CBHW070917160426
43193CB00011B/1500